500 PHR/SHRM-CP Practice Questions With Answers.
Olamide Asekun, PHR.
2016 Edition.

Purpose of This Book.
This book provides accurate information regarding the HR exams in the title above, within the timeframe of its publication.
The federal and state laws discussed in this book are subject to revisions, amendments and judicial revisions that may affect employer or employee laws, rights and obligations.
All rights reserved Copyright 2016.
Introduction.
This book will help you in your PHR/SHRM-CP exam preparations immensely. This is because it is not an exam simulation as the questions have the answers underlined to help you register correct answers. However, the alternatives are probably more relevant to your study than the answers. I will advice that you seek to understand the alternatives. There are tons of questions with "except" which seeks to know if you have adequate knowledge of the subject matter **AND what doesn't pertain to it.** Don't skip over the alternatives; read and painstakingly go through the process of understanding the entire question.
The following are exam tips that will serve a PHR/SHRM-CP aspirant well;

1. One tip that will help you in your exam is reading the questions twice. Don't be in a hurry. Reading a second time will reveal some critical word that you passed over initially.

2. Another tip is to calm down and take your mind off the exam for a minute and bring it back again. You need a fresh perspective to answer the questions correctly and clearing your mind intermittently will help you achieve this.

3. Use a variety of study resources. Use a study guide, videos, practice questions and exam simulation systems. However, don't fall into information paralysis. Streamline your resources and focus on the study resources you have chosen but by all means, engage your mental, visual and auditory learning processes.

4. Prepare for real world HR experiential questions, so study with resources that provide knowledge of HR experience in the USA. Corporate HR webinars will help in this regard.

5. I put together a blog called **passphr.blogspot.com** with loads of exam success tips. Please check it out. It will prove useful in your preparations.

6. Pray and ask God for favour, commit your exams into the hands of the Lord Jesus. Please note, prayer does not take the place of hard-work. Do not be slothful, read overnight, put aside distractions and discipline yourself.

I wish you success!
Olamide Asekun.

1. Disparate impact means?
    a. when a women is required to take tests that men are not required to.
    b. When an Asian is assumed to be smarter than an Hispanic.
    c. <u>Seemingly fair practices that have an adverse effect on a protected class.</u>
    d. The legal right to ask an employee to resign, with or without reason.

2. Which of the following is true about the following labor legislation;
    a. Sherman Antitrust Act of 1890 - It allowed injunctions to forbid groups that conspired to restrain trade.
    b. Norris-La Guardia Act of 1932 - protected the rights of workers to organize and strike without the interference of federal injunctions.
    c. NLRA or Wagner Act of 1935 - identified the 5 employer unfair labor practices.
    d. <u>All of the above.</u>

3. The following are performance review methods except;
    a. <u>Educational.</u>
    b. Narrative.
    c. Rating
    d. Comparison.

4. HR risks can be classified in the following areas except;
    a. Legal Compliance.
    b. Security.
    c. <u>Workplace monitoring.</u>
    d. Business continuity.

5. The Drug-Free Workplace Act of 1970 applies to businesses with federal contracts of $100,000 or more each year. What is inaccurate in this statement?
    a. The Act was established for state contractors not federal contractors.
    b. <u>The Act was established in 1988 not 1970.</u>
    c. The statement is accurate.
    d. The Act applies to businesses with federal contracts worth $50,000.

6. The Labor-Management Relations Act (LMRA) of 1947 established the following except;
    a. <u>It gave employees the right to sue the union.</u>
    b. The LMRA prohibits closed shops and allows union shops only with the consent of employee majority.
    c. It prohibited jurisdictional strikes and secondary boycotts.
    d. The LMRA allows employers to permanently replace striking union workers.

7. Which of the following is considered a business continuity risk?
    a. Environmental disasters.
    b. Organized disruptions.

c. Hacking of business information systems.
   d. All of the above.

8. The following are unlawful activities that could pose a HR risk to an organisation with regard to legal compliance except;
   a. Discrimination.
   b. Ergonomic strains.
   c. Sexual harassment.
   d. Negligent hiring.

9. HR risks with regard to workplace privacy includes which of the following;
   a. Identity theft.
   b. Natural disaster.
   c. Priority disruptions.
   d. Hacking information assets.

10. A bell curve ranking method means;
    a. Rating a small group of employees at a high scale, a small group at the bottom scale and the majority at an average scale.
    b. Rating a large group of employees both at the top and bottom, with a small number of employees at the average scale.
    c. Rating employees as low as possible.
    d. Rating employees as high as possible.

11. Which of the following is NOT a HR risk with regard to Safety and Health?
    a. Ergonomic strains.
    b. Repetitive stress injuries.
    c. System failures.
    d. Workplace injuries,

12. All of these are true about an HR audit except;
    a. It determines the HR practices to continue or discontinue.
    b. It is a key means of measuring HR effectiveness.
    c. It positions HR as a business partner.
    d. It is not effective when outsourced.

13. The HR tools used to identify and assess risks are?
    a. Workplace investigation.
    b. HR Audits.
    c. HR Risk management.
    d. A and B.

14. The union at ANAT company wants to receive automatic deductions as union dues. To be enforceable, what must happen?
    a. The union must get permission from the NLRB.
    b. The union must get permission from the employees.
    c. The employees must give written authorization for the deductions.
    d. Members of the union agree to deductions when they decide to have a union.

15. An HR audit in the compensation and benefits functional area will NOT assess which of the following;
    a. Structure of the HR department.
    b. Consistency of compensation philosophy.
    c. Wage compression.
    d. Health-care cost review.

16. A totality agreement means;
    a. A zipper clause.
    b. A clause which states that the CBA is the entire agreement between the parties.
    c. A and B.
    d. A reform of the LMRA.

17. The TIE company is conducting an HR audit of the Employee Relations department only. What is likely to be assessed?
    a. Conflict-resolution processes.
    b. Turnover demographics.
    c. Diversity practices.
    d. All of the above.

18. Which of the following determines if the NLRB will consider an acquiring owner to be a successor employer?
    a. Substantial continuity of operations.
    b. Similarity of operations and products.
    c. All of the above.
    d. None of the above.

19. An HR audit focused only on recruitment practices, affirmative action programs and labor market demographics is most likely on which of these functional areas;
    a. Organization of HR Function.
    b. Labor relations.
    c. HR Risk management.
    d. Workforce planning and employment.

20. The following are true about the work stoppages listed below except;
    a. Lockouts- when management shuts down operations.

b. <u>Boycotts-when management avoids negotiations.</u>
   c. Strikes- when the union decides to stop working.
   d. All of the above.

21. Why should an HR audit focus on pre-employment tests?
    a. To ensure the tests are valid and reliable.
    b. To abide by the Uniform Guidelines on Employee Selection Procedures.
    c. <u>A and B only.</u>
    d. To determine if alternative staffing methods are required.

22. An unlawful strike in which employees stop working and stay in the building is called;
    a. <u>Sit-down strike.</u>
    b. Work stoppage.
    c. Economic strike.
    d. Work slowdown.

23. Contractors must do the following to be in compliance with the Drug-Free Workplace Act of 1988 except;
    a. Develop a written policy stating they provide a drug-free workplace.
    b. Develop a program to educate employees about the dangers of drug abuse.
    c. Establish penalties for illegal drug convictions.
    d. <u>Develop injunctions according to OSHA's dictates.</u>

24. Mark Harris owns two companies, one is unionized, the other is not unionized. This can be referred to as;
    a. Secondary boycott.
    b. Alter Ego doctrine.
    c. <u>Double-breasting.</u>
    d. Ally doctrine.

25. The Occupational Safety and Health Act (OSHA) established 3 duties for the workplace, which of the following is not one of them?
    a. Employers must provide a workplace free from recognized hazards.
    b. <u>Employees must research and evaluate workplace hazards.</u>
    c. Employers must comply with all safety and health standards.
    d. Employees must comply with occupational safety and health standards.

26. When an employer whose workers are on strike contacts a neutral employer to perform the work of the striking workers, this can be referred to as;
    a. Alter Ego doctrine.
    b. <u>Ally doctrine.</u>
    c. LMRA boycotts.
    d. Unfair Labour Practice.

27. When an employer has two businesses with substantially identical management, operations and ownership, this known as;
   a. <u>Alter Ego employer.</u>
   b. Ally employer.
   c. Double-breasting.
   d. Mediation.

28. The HR Manager of the GRIT company is concerned as a company whose operations complements the operations of the GRIT company is suffering a strike by its union. The GRIT company is involved in;
   a. <u>Straight-line operations.</u>
   b. Boycotting.
   c. Yellow-dog contracts.
   d. Contract clauses.

29. The HR Manager of YET company recently informed the union members that secondary boycotts are ULPs. What is a secondary boycott?
   a. When a union intends to go on strike.
   b. When a union intends to picket.
   c. <u>When a union tries to compel an employer to stop doing business with an employer the union has a dispute with.</u>
   d. None of the above.

30. What is a wildcat strike?
   a. A strike in response to a ULP violation.
   b. <u>Unannounced industrial action in violation of a contract clause prohibiting strikes.</u>
   c. A strike in support of a hot-cargo clause.
   d. A strike against a hot-cargo clause.

31. The Labor Management Reporting and Disclosure Act (LMRDA) of 1959 established which of the following;
   a. It placed controls on internal union operations.
   b. It restricted increases in union dues and extortionate picketing.
   c. It provides safeguards against retaliatory disciplinary actions by the union.
   d. <u>All of the above.</u>

32. Which of these is the most important reason why performance appraisals should be documented?
   a. To ensure employees perform their duties as at when due.
   b. To serve as a structures means of communication.
   c. <u>To help defend employment actions, positive or negative.</u>
   d. To provide performance feedback.

33. The REEG company's union has embarked on a strike to obtain better pay and working conditions, this strike is;
    a. Unlawful and economic.
    b. Lawful and economic.
    c. An unfair labor practices.
    d. AN NLRB infraction.

34. Discriminatory hiring actions can be allowed under Title VII in which case;
    a. Legitimate seniority
    b. Discriminatory hiring actions are not allowed under Title VII
    c. Influence on corporate leadership
    d. Bona fide Occupational Qualifications (BFOQ)

35. The following makes a strike unlawful except?
    a. If it occurs in response to an employer unfair labor practice.
    b. If it supports union unfair labor practices.
    c. If the strikers engage in serious misconduct.
    d. If it violates a no-strike clause in the contract.

36. A best practice in performance appraisal is;
    a. For supervisors to provide constant feedback to employees.
    b. Communicate performance expectations clearly.
    c. Set goals for the next review period.
    d. All of the above.

37. The CEO of LIN company has informed employees that joining a union may hinder promotion chances. This is an example of ;
    a. Intimidation.
    b. Exaggeration.
    c. Unfair Labor Practices.
    d. Prohibitive activities.

38. An example of lobbying is;
    a. A member of congress sponsors a bill
    b. A non-profit organisation finds a sponsor for a bill.
    c. A congress committee conducts an approval for a bill.
    d. A senator seeks presidential backing on a bill.

39. An action that restrains or coerces employees from exercising rights to organize or bargain collectively is;
    a. Unfair Labor Practice.
    b. No-strike clause.

c. Labor coercion.
   d. Anti-NLRB.

40. In the case of Stender v. Lucky Stores, which of these is true;
    a. The HR team were found culpable of negligent hiring.
    b. A lawsuit on gender discrimination was filed following information from a diversity training.
    c. A lawsuit on repatriation of non-US citizens.
    d. Flexible work arrangements were found to be discriminatory.

41. The acronym TIPS helps to make sure employers avoid prohibited labor activity. What does TIPS stand for?
    a. Threaten, Indict, Promise and Spy on employees.
    b. Threaten, Interrogate, Promise or Spy on employees.
    c. Threaten, Interrogate, Propagate and Spy on employees.
    d. Threaten, Investigate, Promise or Spy on employees

42. The Rehabilitation Act of 1973 is all these except;
    a. Prohibits discrimination on the basis of disability in programs run by all agencies.
    b. Covers federal contractors with contracts of $10,000+.
    c. Requires federal information technology to be accessible to people with disabilities.
    d. Prohibits federal employers from discriminating against qualified people with disabilities.

43. Employers must not enter into a hot-cargo agreement. What is a hot-cargo agreement?
    a. An importation clause.
    b. Union organizing.
    c. When at the union's request, employers stop doing business with another employer.
    d. Refusing to bargain in good faith.

44. The following are crucial to an effective repatriation program except;
    a. Assistance in managing the transition to and from the host country.
    b. Effective repatriate knowledge management.
    c. Provide employment for the employee's spouse.
    d. One-on-one debrief between the manager and repatriate.

45. Featherbedding is a ULP, what does it mean?
    a. When unions require employers to keep employees on jobs rendered obsolete by technology.
    b. Restrain manager's ability to discipline union members.
    c. Turn a blind eye to union excessive dues and membership fees.
    d. Featherbedding is a legal term for administrative law court corruption.

46. The RTT corporation is being investigated for discriminatory promotion practices. The company HRIS will be helpful to;
    a. Provide trends and ratio analyses of the company's promotion processes.
    b. Provide data related to the corporation's affirmative action processes.
    c. Provide summary comparison of promotion forecast.
    d. Provide data on the EEO-1 and OFCCP compliance forms.

47. In which of these instances is picketing unlawful?
    a. When another union has been lawfully recognized as the bargaining representative.
    b. When a representation election was held within the previous 12 months.
    c. When a representation election is not filed within 30 days of the start of the picketing.
    d. All of the above.

48. Job reinforcement is critical to;
    a. Effective transfer of training.
    b. Supervisory authority.
    c. Negative accelerating curve.
    d. Change increments.

49. Yellow dog contracts entails which of the following?
    a. Employers used yellow-dog contracts to prevent employees from joining unions by signing agreements.
    b. The agreement stipulates that joining a union in the future will be sufficient grounds for dismissal.
    c. A and B.
    d. None of the above.

50. The ADAAA defined disability as an impairment that substantially limits one or more major life activities. The following are correct under the ADAAA except;
    a. Specified that disability includes any impairment that is in remission if it will substantially limit a life activity when active.
    b. Reasonable accommodation must be provided for individuals who have substance abuse issues.
    c. Prohibits consideration of ameliorative effects of mitigating measures when assessing an impairment.
    d. Major life activities is expanded to include major bodily functions.

51. The following are NLRB remedies when an Employer engages in ULPs except?
    a. Disband an employer-dominated union.
    b. Engage in the collective bargaining process.
    c. Change company ownership.
    d. Reinstate employees to positions held prior to the ULP.

52. What is the training cost for each employee in this scenario; $5,000 was spent for the training, $1,000 for the training location; 30 full-time employees (40 hours/week) and 4 part-time employees (20 hours/week).
    a. $200.
    b. $187.50
    c. $155.50.
    d. $147.50.

53. The following are NLRB remedies when a Union engages in ULPs except?
    a. Refund excessive dues with interest to members.
    b. Engage in the collective bargaining process.
    c. Sign a written agreement with the employer.
    d. Disband the union.

54. Company TIC has embarked on a survey on customer satisfaction with their detergent range. This survey was sent to 3,000 of the current estimate of 5,000 customers. Company TIC is using;
    a. A sample.
    b. A distribution.
    c. A prerequisite population
    d. The top customers.

55. ULPs must be filed to the NLRB within how many months of the incident?
    a. 3 months.
    b. 6 months.
    c. Immediately the incident occurred.
    d. 9 months.

56. Monetary compensation includes the following except;
    a. 401(k) matching.
    b. Pension plans.
    c. Employee Stock Ownership Programs (ESOPs).
    d. Intrinsic rewards.

57. Groups of employees strongly challenge supervisors about benefits and employment practices. What is likely happening?
    a. Picketing.
    b. Union organizing.
    c. Impending strike.
    d. NLRB elections.

58. The Age Discrimination in Employment Act of 1967 (ADEA) stipulates the following except;
    a. The ADEA overrides the procedures of hiring of firefighters and police officers.

b. Prohibits discrimination against persons 40 years of age or older.
c. The ADEA applies to businesses with more than 20 employees.
d. Waiver of rights must include a period of 21 days to review the waiver.

59. Which of these is not a part of the union recognition process?
    a. Signing of authorization cards.
    b. Demand for recognition.
    c. <u>Petition to LMRA for elections.</u>
    d. Election.

60. Non-monetary compensation includes the following except;
    a. Telecommuting.
    b. Flex-time.
    c. Recognition.
    d. <u>**Direct compensation.**</u>

61. The NLRB will hold an election if how many percent of cards are signed?
    a. <u>**30% of the eligible employees.**</u>
    b. 50% of the eligible employees.
    c. 25% of the eligible employees.
    d. 30% of all employees.

62. The following will be assessed in an HR audit except;
    a. <u>**Strategic planning.**</u>
    b. Benefits and compensation.
    c. FLSA compliance.
    d. HRIS system.

63. Wayne, the HR Supervisor has agreed to a neutrality agreement with the union before realizing he is not sure what it means? Can you help Wayne?
    a. It means the employer has agreed to a NLRB election.
    b. <u>**It means the employer has agreed not to say or do anything in opposition to the union.**</u>
    c. It means the employer is neutral to union ULPs.
    d. None of the above.

64. Any employee payment not associated with wages and salaries is known as;
    a. Non-monetary compensation.
    b. Social Society benefits.
    c. <u>**Indirect compensation.**</u>
    d. Internal payments.

65. When an employer agrees to recognize a union based on signed authorization cards, this is called?

a. Easy recognition.
b. Unionization.
c. Black-dog agreements.
d. <u>Card-check election.</u>

66. Which of the following is correct under the ADEA?
   a. Waivers of rights and waivers involving exits have the same considerations.
   b. The ADEA protects against discharge or discipline for just cause.
   c. <u>Waivers on exits or termination require 45 days to consider the agreement.</u>
   d. ADEA does not provide for BFOQs to the business operations.

67. The NLRB in devising a bargaining unit seeks to determine if there is a "community of interest" in the unit. What does this mean?
   a. <u>To ensure the interests of the unit members are sufficiently similar.</u>
   b. To ensure the unit is not a fictional arrangement.
   c. To ensure bickerings do not ensue.
   d. None of the above.

68. Which of these is an important aspect of a Total Rewards Program?
   a. <u>Differentiating jobs.</u>
   b. Business risks.
   c. Managerial constraints.
   d. An annual bonus.

69. Which of these employees are not eligible for inclusion in bargaining units?
   a. Management personnel.
   b. Independent contractors.
   c. Supervisors.
   d. <u>All of the above.</u>

70. An employee informs his wife that a top product will be introduced by his company and based on this information, his wife buys stock in the company. What ethical violation has occurred?
   a. Fiduciary mismanagement.
   b. Conflict of interest.
   c. Position abuse.
   d. <u>Insider trading.</u>

71. The following is true about Procedural Justice except;
   a. The perception of fairness in determining pay processes and procedures.
   b. Perception on how pay rates are determined.
   c. Perception on how bonuses are distributed.
   d. <u>Perception on how pay reflects actual performance.</u>

72. A type of budgeting where executives begin with a clear slate and must justify expenses is called;
    a. Historical budgeting.
    b. <u>Zero-based budgeting.</u>
    c. Formula-based budgeting.
    d. Correlation budgeting.

73. Ann is a super performer and always exceeds performance expectations. Rose on the other hand has a significant lower level of productivity. Due to this, Ann's pay is higher than Rose's even though they are on the same pay scale. Which of these applies to the case above;
    a. <u>Distributive justice.</u>
    b. Personal bias.
    c. Procedural justice.
    d. Ineffective total rewards policies.

74. Title VII of 1964 identified five protected classes, these are
    a. Race, Color, Religion, Sex, Tribe
    b. <u>Color, Gender, Religion, Race, National origin</u>
    c. Religion, Sexuality, Gender, Religion, Country
    d. National Origin, Sex, Color, Class, Religion

75. When pay systems can be justified via job-related criteria and industry/external market conditions, the company is said to have;
    a. Pay sensitivity.
    b. <u>Pay equity.</u>
    c. Compensation strategy.
    d. Open pay.

76. The information technology department in organisations are seen as strategic partners majorly due to;
    a. Outsourcing technology has prohibitive costs.
    b. IT employees can train the entire organisation.
    c. IT employees can enrich the organisation by developing softwares.
    d. <u>Technology can serve as a competitive advantage for an organisation.</u>

77. Pay openness refers to;
    a. <u>The degree of secrecy around pay.</u>
    b. The inability of HR to keep pay records confidential.
    c. Internal equity.
    d. A pay-for-performance criteria.

78. This are all true about FEPA except;

- a. FEPA means Fair Employment Practices Agencies.
- b. FEPA are agencies of the states to enforce EEO legislation.
- **c. FEPA decisions override EEOC decisions.**
- d. Individuals may file with either FEPA or EEOC.

79. Which of these total rewards philosophy is best for an organization that places premium value on employee longevity?
    - a. Performance-based philosophy.
    - **b. Entitlement philosophy.**
    - c. Sedimentary philosophy.
    - d. Line of sight.

80. What is the preferred method for a HR Professional to protect a company against identified risks?
    - **a. Obtain employment practices liability insurance.**
    - b. Request for an OFCCP inspection.
    - c. Educate staff about risk avoidance.
    - d. Create an environment of accountability.

81. The SEC requires that annual compensation for the top five executives be reported. The information required includes the following except;
    - a. Deferred compensation.
    - b. Executive pensions.
    - c. Cash compensation.
    - **d. Market data.**

82. Reasonable accommodation means;
    - a. Provide accessible facilities to persons with disabilities.
    - b. Job requirements be adjusted to accommodate qualified persons with disabilities.
    - c. Provide vision enabling technology for employees.
    - **d. A & B.**

83. The following are ways an HR professional can breach a fiduciary responsibility except?
    - a. Acting in self-interest.
    - b. Conflicting duties.
    - **c. Fault-finding.**
    - d. Personal profiting.

84. Which of these structures will be appropriate for a company whose sales come from 4 key commodities?
    - a. Floorboard structure.
    - b. Hierarchical structure.
    - **c. Product-based structure.**

d. Functional structure.

85. Line of sight occurs when employees know that their performance impacts pay. Which of these is not true?
    a. Line of sight can help create a high performance culture.
    b. Line of sight helps to achieve company goals.
    c. <u>Line of sight is effective for all compensation philosophies.</u>
    d. Line of sight is used in a performance-based culture.

86. The Surge Company has declared that accommodation for an electronic wheelchair with laser technology for a disabled employee constitutes an "undue hardship". What is an undue hardship?
    a. An accommodation that is of huge cost.
    b. <u>An accommodation that places an excessive burden on the employer.</u>
    c. An accommodation that due to size, is impossible to provide.
    d. An accommodation that impacts the financial resources of the organization.

87. The FLSA established the following requirements except;
    a. Introduced minimum wage.
    b. Determined criteria for exempt jobs.
    c. <u>Ensures children do not work.</u>
    d. Determined overtime payments requirements.

88. The most frequent OSHA violation citation is in what industry;
    a. <u>Construction.</u>
    b. Education.
    c. Textile.
    d. Whistleblower.

89. According to the FLSA, what does exempt mean?
    a. Not applicable to FLSA.
    b. Not identified under the FLSA.
    c. Determination of job responsibilities.
    d. <u>Defining the pay status of all positions to determine if certain FLSA components such as overtime, apply or not.</u>

90. The EEOC regulates compliance of the following areas except;
    a. Age.
    b. Genetic Information.
    c. Pregnancy.
    d. <u>Minimum wage.</u>

91. What is a hot-cargo clause?

a. A clause where the employer requires that employees sign an agreement not to join a union.
   b. <u>A clause prohibiting an employer from conducting business with some other person with whom the union has or may have a dispute.</u>
   c. A clause only valid in the healthcare industry.
   d. None of the above.

92. Police officers and firefighters employed by small departments of fewer than five employees are exempt from;
   a. <u>Overtime requirement.</u>
   b. Minimum wage requirement.
   c. Exempt requirement.
   d. Labor requirement.

93. In the construction industry, a union shop clause requires that all employees join the union within a grace period of how many days?
   a. 30 days.
   b. 10 days.
   c. <u>7 days.</u>
   d. 21 days.

94. Employee pension rights are protected by which of the following?
   a. OFCCP.
   b. <u>USERRA.</u>
   c. Sherman Antitrust Act.
   d. ADEA.

95. A clause that allows employees to choose whether to join the union but once they join, they must remain members till the contract expires is called;
   a. <u>Maintenance of membership clause.</u>
   b. Union shop clause.
   c. Agency shop clause.
   d. Closed shop clause.

96. Newspaper delivery jobs are exempt from which of the following;
   a. Minimum wage.
   b. Overtime.
   c. Child labour.
   d. <u>All of the above.</u>

97. A closed shop clause requires that all new hires be members of the union BEFORE they're hired. Is the closed shop clause legal?
   a. <u>Only in the construction industry.</u>

b. Yes, it is.
c. No, it isn't.
d. Only in the architectural industry

98. Rita participated in an employment discrimination proceeding which ended in a $10,000 fine for the company Rita works with. After 2 months, Rita was fired for insubordination. Under which of the following can Rita file a charge to the EEOC?
   a. Discrimination
   b. Retaliation.
   c. Examination protection.
   d. Sexual Harassment.

99. The CEO of an airline company is negotiating for a no strike/no lockout clause in the collective bargaining agreement because in his view "the clause is mutually beneficial". Which of the following best explains this?
   a. The clause is best for employers only.
   b. The clause provides economic protection from work stoppages which will affect both sides adversely.
   c. The CEO is committing a ULP.
   d. None of the above.

100. Employees must be paid a minimum salary of $--- per week, or $--- per year in the salary level test of the FLSA exemption requirement:
   a. $455; 23,660.
   b. $435; 23,660.
   c. $455, 23,360.
   d. $435; 23,360.

101. An inventory management system which states "purchase smaller amounts of supplies frequently" is called;
   a. SMART inventory.
   b. Just-in-time inventory.
   c. Restrictive inventory.
   d. Blanket inventory.

102. Which of the following is true about the "salary basis" test to determine exemption test?
   a. Employees' payment is predetermined and on a regular set schedule.
   b. Employee's compensation cannot be reduced because of work variations.
   c. Employee must be paid a full salary if any work is performed.
   d. All of the above.

103. Which of these is an example of "Reverse Discrimination"?
   a. When a staff uses the EEOC to discriminate against an employer.

b. When the EEOC is found culpable in a discrimination charge.
c. <u>When staff without disability use the ADA to file claims because disabled individuals receive favourable employment actions.</u>
d. When individuals can demonstrate that their employers have ignored the mitigating measure doctrine.

104. For ----- to qualify for exemption, they will be paid $455 per week or $27.63 per hour.
   a. <u>Computer professionals.</u>
   b. Status professionals.
   c. Industry experts.
   d. None of the above.

105. Determining the job requirements of a position for the purpose of defining exemption status is known as;
   a. Job exposition.
   b. <u>Duties test.</u>
   c. Criterion validity.
   d. Constructive validity.

106. The lowest remuneration that employers may legally pay to workers or the price below which workers may not sell their labor is called;
   a. Exempt wages.
   b. Non-exempt wages.
   c. <u>Minimum wage.</u>
   d. Fair labour wages.

107. ADA compliance includes;
   a. Engaging in an interactive process with disabled individuals on treatment of ailments.
   b. Engaging with other employees on accommodating the excesses of disabled individuals.
   c. <u>Engaging and interacting with disabled individuals on requests of reasonable accommodation.</u>
   d. Engaging disabled individuals on negligent hiring.

108. Which of the following statements about minimum wage is correct?
   a. Where the state minimum wage is higher than the federal government, the state requirement supersedes the federal minimum wage.
   b. Where the state minimum wage is lower than the federal government, the federal minimum wage supersedes the state requirements.
   c. Non-exempt employees must be paid at least the minimum wage for all compensable time.
   d. <u>All of the above.</u>

109. Some employees have been acting disgruntled and having private conversations in the break room. What is likely happening?
   a. An upcoming strike.
   b. Union organizing.
   c. Yellow dog contracts.
   d. Union pre-election activities.

110. Ana resumes as a HR trainee in the Lift Inc. You have been asked to train her on overtime, which of the following is incorrect overtime information to teach Ana?
   a. Overtime pay is calculated for nonexempt employees as one and a half of the regular wage rate.
   b. If an employee's pay is $20/hour and works for 3 hours overtime, he/she will receive $90 appr. as overtime pay.
   c. Overtime pay is twice the regular pay.
   d. Compensatory time-off can be used instead of overtime payment by public employers only.

111. When some employees on the 3rd shift are paid $0.50 more than employees on other shifts. This is known as;
   a. Bonus pay.
   b. Pay differential.
   c. Shift pay.
   d. Duration pay.

112. Tim is given a 15 minutes break at work with the understanding that this break shall not be paid for, is this correct according to the FLSA?
   a. Yes, his break is not overtime or minimum wage so it is not compensable.
   b. Yes, the FLSA states that breaks less than 20 minutes are not compensable.
   c. No, the FLSA states that breaks less than 20 minutes are compensable.
   d. No, the FLSA states that all breaks are compensable.

113. In which of the following is travel time compensable?
   a. Emergency travel from home to work.
   b. One-day off-site assignments outside regular worksite.
   c. Work travel away from home that spans overnight.
   d. All of the above.

114. Which of the following information about federal employment legislation is incorrect?
   a. Davis-Bacon Act (1931) - pay prevailing wage for local area; applies to federal construction contracts of $2,000 or more.
   b. Walsh-Healey Public Contracts Act (1936) - pay prevailing wage for local area; applies to government contracts exceeding $10,000.

c. MCNamara-O'Hara Service Contract Act (1965) - requires that all federal service contractors pay the prevailing wage.
   d. All are incorrect.

115. Dan has travelled overnight on behalf of his company as a passenger on an airplane. Dan has requested for compensation for the time he spent on the flight, is this correct?
   a. **No, the DOL excludes time spent as a passenger on an airplane from compensable time.**
   b. Yes, he was in the company service while on the plane.
   c. No, he is an exempt employee.
   d. Yes, it is defensible under "travel away from home".

116. The Griggs vs Duke Power case in 1971 established the following except;
   a. **The case established that the black employees earned the highest income.**
   b. Job requirement must be shown to be job-related in order to be lawful.
   c. Discrimination doesn't need to be intentional to exist.
   d. The white employees who didn't have high-school diplomas performed well on the job.

117. The following are some of the factors used to determine whether employers have an actual practice of wrong deductions from exempt pay except;
   a. The number of improper deductions compared to the number of employee infractions.
   b. The number of employees affected.
   c. The time period of the deduction.
   d. **The managerial injunctions against the FLSA.**

118. Which of these is not true about the FLSA of 1938?
   a. It covers virtually all employers in the United States.
   b. It includes enterprise and individual coverage.
   c. It regulates overtime and child labor.
   d. **It does not regulate minimum wage.**

119. The Hardi organisation intends to apply the safe-harbor provision with regard to payroll mistakes discovered, what does this mean?
   a. That there is a clearly communicated policy prohibiting improper deductions.
   b. The Hardi organisation will reimburse employees for improper deductions.
   c. A good-faith commitment is considered.
   d. **A and B.**

120. All these are environmental hazards except?
   a. Pesticious hazards.
   b. **Workplace hazards.**
   c. Electrical explosions.
   d. Gas breakages.

121. Which of the following is not a type of exemption classification?
    a. Executive exemption.
    b. Administrative exemption.
    c. Professional exemption.
    d. <u>Required exemption.</u>

122. All these are true about employment test validity except;
    a. Tests that have an adverse impact on a protected class are lawful if they are valid predictors of success on the job.
    b. Tests must be job-related and valid predictors of job performance.
    c. Subjective supervisor rankings are not sufficient for criterion validation.
    d. <u>Tests that have race implications have been expunged by law.</u>

123. The outside sales exemption is different from other white-collar exemptions mainly because;
    a. The employee must make sales and not be an executive.
    b. The employee must be engaged away from the workplace.
    c. <u>There is no salary requirement.</u>
    d. The use of facilities is a consideration for payment.

124. Wages are to base pay as incentives are to?
    a. Bonuses.
    b. <u>Variable pay.</u>
    c. Direct funding.
    d. Indirect compensation.

125. Children of --- and --- age can work in non- farming and non-hazardous outside school hours on a restricted basis.
    a. 10 and 11.
    b. 10 and 13.
    c. 12 and 13.
    d. <u>14 and 15.</u>

126. These legislations are enforced by these agencies except;
    a. Civil Rights - EEOC
    b. Polygraph - Department of Labour (DOL)
    c. Privacy - Department of Justice (DOJ)
    d. <u>Mass Layoffs - EEOC</u>

127. Which time reporting is best suited for nonexempt employees?
    a. Negative time reporting.
    b. <u>Positive time reporting.</u>

c. Exception time reporting.
d. Overtime reporting.

128. There is a mildly injured employee that seems qualified to complete some job functions, which of the following Return-To-Work (RTW) strategies should HR recommend?
    a. <u>An independent medical exam.</u>
    b. Modified duty.
    c. Quality Management.
    d. Clerical tasks.

129. The FLSA requires that certain records be kept accurately by all employers. Which of the following records is not required by the FLSA?
    a. <u>Production layout information.</u>
    b. Total overtime pay for the workweek.
    c. Deductions and addition to wages.
    d. Total hours worked and each work week.

130. The EEOC is to Equal Employment as the FLSA is to
    a. 12 weeks leave.
    b. <u>Overtime.</u>
    c. Affirmative Action.
    d. Age discrimination.

131. When an employer makes an error on the payroll, misclassifies employees as exempt to avoid overtime costs, which of the following is not likely to happen?
    a. Be required to pay retroactive overtime pay.
    b. <u>The EEOC may deny exemption classifications to the company.</u>
    c. Be required to pay penalties to the affected employees.
    d. A government audit of the general pay practices.

132. Non-exempt employees may not be paid to attend training in the following circumstances except;
    a. The event must be outside normal work-hours.
    b. <u>It is involuntary.</u>
    c. It is not job related.
    d. No other work is performed during the event.

133. Employees can recover back wages by one of the following except?
    a. The DOL can supervise the payment of the back wages.
    b. <u>The DOJ can file a lawsuit for the amount of back-wages and liquidated damages.</u>
    c. The employee can file a private lawsuit.
    d. The DOL can file an injunction preventing the employer from unlawfully withholding minimum wage and overtime payments.

134. What is asynchronous training?
   a. Website information training.
   b. Boardroom computer training.
   c. Self-paced training requiring computer control timing protocol.
   d. Rated training.

135. There is a 2-year statute of limitation for back-pay recovery by the FLSA, except for wilful violation which extends to 3 years. What is a statute of limitation?
   a. Penalty on company pay processes and procedures.
   b. Limitation on the autonomy of the employer over overtime and minimum wage decisions.
   c. Amendment duration for rectifying the company's payroll processes.
   d. The maximum time that parties have to initiate legal proceedings from the date of the alleged offense.

136. The EEOA (Equal Employment Opportunity Act) of 1972 established the following except;
   a. Created an Affirmative Action Plan for Equal Employment Opportunities.
   b. Provides litigation authority to the EEOC.
   c. Extended coverage of Title VII to educational institutions, federal, state & local government.
   d. Reduced the employer coverage of the EEOC from 25 to 15 required employees.

137. The following is true about FLSA violations except;
   a. Employers may not terminate employees who file FLSA complaints.
   b. Wilful violators may be fined up to $10, 000.
   c. No FLSA violation can lead to imprisonment.
   d. Employers may be subject to Civil Money Penalty (CMP) of up to $11,000 for each employee on child labor violations.

138. The SEC requires public companies to disclose the compensation of how many executives?
   a. 7.
   b. 5.
   c. All board executives.
   d. The top 3 executives.

139. The Equal Pay Act of 1963 mainly focuses on which of the following;
   a. Equal pay for underground workers.
   b. Prohibits discrimination on the basis of sex.
   c. Equal pay for equal work with similar conditions, skill and responsibilities.
   d. B and C.

140. Rita has taken her employers to court on the basis that the Company doesn't provide a retirement plan. Based on which legislation does Rita have a case?
   a. EEOC.
   b. COBRA.
   c. ERISA.
   d. <u>Retirement benefits are not required by federal law.</u>

141. The Portal to Portal Act of 1947 is mainly about which of the following;
   a. Clarified what was considered to be compensable time.
   b. Established that employers are not required to pay for employee commute time.
   c. Requires employers to pay nonexempt employees who perform regular work duties before or after regular work hours or during lunch breaks.
   d. <u>All of the above.</u>

142. The Equal Pay Act applies to employers and employees covered by the FLSA. Which of the agencies below administers and enforces the Equal Pay Act (EPA);
   a. DOL.
   b. DOJ.
   c. <u>EEOC.</u>
   d. SEC.

143. Genetic Information Nondiscrimination Act of 2008 (GINA) stipulates the following except;
   a. The act prohibits genetic information discrimination in employment.
   b. Strictly limits the disclosure of genetic information
   c. <u>The act penalizes employers for inadvertently obtaining genetic information.</u>
   d. Genetic information may be disclosed to employers if it doesn't identify specific employees.

144. Which of the following is not true about Seniority-based compensation?
   a. Annual increases are determined by seniority.
   b. Companies with union representation usually have a seniority based compensation.
   c. It represents an entitlement compensation philosophy.
   d. <u>Compensation is based on merit.</u>

145. Which court case established that union members have a right to representation at meetings where discipline may occur?
   a. Griggs v. Duke Company.
   b. <u>NLRB v. J.Weingarten, Inc.</u>
   c. NLRB v. Davis.
   d. NLRB v. Nissan Inc.

146. Pay differential is additional pay for work that is considered beyond the minimum requirements of the job. Which of these is not an example of pay differentials;

a. Hazard pay.
   b. Incentive pay.
   c. Geographic pay.
   d. Overtime.

147. Vietnam Era Veterans' Readjustment Assistance Act of 1974 (VEVRAA) applies to the following except;
   a. Applies to federal contractors or subcontractors with contracts of $25,000 or more.
   b. Requires federal contractors to list all job openings with state employment agencies.
   c. VEVRAA has exceptions of senior-level management positions, positions filled from within and positions lasting 3 days or less.
   d. All VEVRAA positions must be published in the Federal Register of Veterans.

148. Anna works in a hazardous chemical environment. She works 40 hours in a week. In the preceding week, Anna worked for 32 hours (Tuesday - Friday) because Monday was a public holiday. Anna worked for 8 hours on Saturday as well. Is Anna entitled to overtime for her work on Saturday?
   a. No, the FLSA requires payment only for overtime exceeding 40 hours in a week, Anna worked for 40 hours in the week.
   b. Yes, Anna doesn't work on Saturday and should be paid 1.5 her hourly rate for the 8 hours worked.
   c. No, Anna works in a hazardous environment and is being paid hazard pay which qualifies for overtime as well.
   d. Yes, Anna should be paid hazard pay, shift premium (10%) and overtime pay which is 1.5 her hourly rate.

149. Decertification means;
   a. When employees call for an election for a change in management.
   b. When employees call for an election so the union can represent them.
   c. When employees call for an election so the union no longer represents them.
   d. When a contract bar is deauthorized.

150. What is variable compensation;
   a. Compensation that is cash-based and regular.
   b. Compensation based on employee performance and/or organizational results.
   c. Compensation that varies from industry to industry.
   d. Compensation based on geographic differentials.

151. Executive orders are best defined as;
   a. Presidential proclamations through the Congress which becomes law after 20 days.
   b. Presidential proclamations that ensure equal employment opportunities.
   c. Presidential proclamations published in the Federal Register.

d. Presidential proclamations published in the Federal Register which become law after 30 days.

152. Individual incentives have three critical phases. Which of these is not correct about the 3 critical phases?
   a. Plan Design -an example is "increase production by 20%, receive a bonus of 10%".
   b. Review Process -Review bonus payment and company's "ability to pay".
   c. Gainsharing -Sharing the benefits of success.
   d. Communication & Implementation.

153. A legislative committee is set up to do which of the following;
   a. To sponsor a bill.
   b. To study and determine if a bill will get a pass vote by Congress.
   c. To engage lobbyists before bills are submitted to Congress.
   d. To support the passage of a bill.

154. The following are group incentives except;
   a. Profit-sharing.
   b. Bonus.
   c. Employee Stock Purchase Plan.
   d. Improshare.

155. Executive orders relating to equal employment issues are enforced by the;
   a. EEOC.
   b. OFCCP.
   c. DOL.
   d. DOJ.

156. Which of these is not true about these gainsharing programs;
   a. Improshare - Standard hours are calculated for the production of each unit, and improshare pays a bonus when the time needed in the production process is reduced.
   b. Scanlon Plan - employees share in pre-established cost savings, based upon employee effort.
   c. Profit-sharing -a system in which the people who work for a company receive a direct share of the profits, usually on an annual basis.
   d. Employee Stock Ownership Plans (ESOP) and Employee Stock Purchase Plan (ESPP) are vested after 3 years.

157. Total Quality Management is an intervention that focuses on;
   a. Employee needs.
   b. Reduce waste.
   c. Revenue generation.
   d. Customer needs.

158. Which of these is not true about ESOPs and ESPPs?
   a. ESOPs and ESPPs are not tax-deductible.
   b. ESPPs purchase company stock at a discount rate of up to 15%.
   c. Employees must be 100% vested in their stock within three to six years.
   d. The programs help build a culture of employee ownership and loyalty.

159. The Executive Orders below relates to the following issues except;
   a. Executive Order 11246 - Prohibits employment discrimination on the basis of race, creed, color or national origin.
   b. Executive Order 11375 - Expanded coverage for protected classes to include discrimination based on sex.
   c. Executive Order 12138 - added the "status of parent" to the list of protected classes.
   d. Executive Order 13087 - Expanded coverage to include sexual orientation.

160. Which of these is not true about Job Evaluation (JE)?
   a. Job evaluations seeks to determine the value of jobs relative to each other.
   b. Job evaluations are the first step to defining ERISA compliance.
   c. Job evaluations are conducted when a job is developed or duties change.
   d. Job evaluations identify and define compensable factors of a job.

161. Which of these is not true about vesting?
   a. Vesting rules are backed by the EEOA of 1973.
   b. Vesting means the employee has earned the right to benefits without the risk of forfeiting them.
   c. Cliff vesting is when employees are 100% vested after specified years of service.
   d. Gradual vesting is when employees become 20% vested after 3 years until they are 100% vested after 7 years of service.

162. Which of these patents protect new designs for 14 years?
   a. Commodity patents.
   b. Creative patents.
   c. Design patents.
   d. Utility patents.

163. The RATA company uses a job evaluation method where the value of jobs are compared to one another. Managers conduct the job evaluations which makes the process cost-effective. However, it has been difficult to compare unrelated jobs and there have been murmurings of subjectivity in the process. The RATA company is using which job evaluation method;
   a. Ranking Method.
   b. Hay Point System.
   c. Point Factor System.
   d. Rating Method.

164. The two levels of compliance required by Executive Orders are;
    a. This level prohibits employment discrimination and requires contractors to take affirmative action in employment actions, in contracts totaling $10,000 or more in a 12 month period.
    b. <u>A and C.</u>
    c. This level is for contractors with 50 or more employees who have contracts of $50,000 or more are required to have a written Affirmative Action Plan (AAP) and be developed within 120 days of the contract with the OFCCP.
    d. This level requires that tax-exempt companies submit the EEO-1 form by September 30 annually.

165. The GAIR company CEO wants an overhauling on the Job Evaluation Method. He has requested for a method that benchmarks positions to determine internal equity. The GAIR CEO is NOT likely to implement which of these Job Evaluation Methods?
    a. Point Factor.
    b. <u>Ranking System.</u>
    c. Hay System.
    d. Classification Method.

166. When professional colleagues work together to reflect on current practices, refine and build new skills as well as share ideas, this is called?
    a. Mentoring.
    b. Strategic training.
    c. <u>Peer to peer coaching.</u>
    d. Executive coaching.

167. The Point Factor and Hay System are examples of:
    a. Composition Method.
    b. Ranking Method.
    c. <u>Job Evaluation Classification Method.</u>
    d. None of the above.

168. If an employee was born 1960 or later, the full retirement age is;
    a. 65.
    b. 62.
    c. <u>67.</u>
    d. 60.

169. All these are true about the EEO-1 report except;
    a. The report was developed by the EEOC and the OFCCP.
    b. The report requires employers to provide a count of their employees by job category, ethnicity, race and gender.

c. There are no job categories required on the EEO-1 report form.
  d. The report forms the basis of Affirmative Action Plans.

170. Job pricing is used to ensure pay is competitive. The following are steps to job pricing except;
  a. Review job description.
  b. Salary commissions.
  c. Review compensation components.
  d. Recommend salary range.

171. A discretionary amount of money added to wages, usually as a reward for good performance is called;
  a. Pay incentive.
  b. Pay increase.
  c. Bonus.
  d. Commission.

172. Which of the following is not a type of salary survey?
  a. Employer survey.
  b. Government survey.
  c. Industry survey.
  d. Commissioned survey.

173. Who must file the EEO-1 report?
  a. All federal agencies.
  b. Employers with federal government contracts of $50,000+ & 50+ employees.
  c. Employers who do not have a federal government contract but have 100+ employees.
  d. B & C.

174. The High-Tech company wants to gather compensation and benefits data about specific competitors that have head-hunted their top executives. What salary survey would be best for the High-Tech company's needs?
  a. Peculiar survey.
  b. Commissioned survey.
  c. Participatory survey.
  d. Exclusive survey.

175. When a union representative request copies of incident reports filed annually, what is HR legally required to do?
  a. Provide the copies of the "tell us about the case" within 7 calendar days.
  b. Refuse to provide the reports except an OSHA inspection has taken place.
  c. Provide the copies within 15 calendar days.
  d. Only provide the "tell us about the case" copies within 3 days.

176. Tina has a presentation on her company's salary structure to new employees. One of the employees asks Tina what a salary/pay range is. What is Tina's best response?
   a. The question is beyond the scope of the class.
   b. A salary/ pay range is the span between the minimum and maximum base salary an organization will pay for a specific job or group of jobs.
   c. A salary/pay range is the midpoint progression of consecutive grades of jobs.
   d. Pay information is legally required to be confidential.

Use the Case Below To answer Questions 177 - 179.

177. The TIG company management has received a complaint that the Head of Operations has sexually harassed a temporary employee. Also, exit interviews indicate constructive discharge claims against him. Which of the following tools should be used in this case;
   a. The corporate disciplinary process.
   b. Peer to Peer Review.
   c. Workplace Investigation.
   d. HR Audit.

178. How would you advise that the TIG company (the case above) investigate the accusations above, given that the Head of Human Resources reports to the Head of Operations?
   a. Through a third party investigator.
   b. Through the Head of HR.
   c. Hand the case over to the EEOC.
   d. Hand the case over to the police.

179. The best practice for an investigator who intends to conduct interviews on the complaints raised against the Head of Operations is:
   a. Interview the accused; witnesses; complainant.
   b. Interview the complainant; witnesses; accused.
   c. Interview all three together for avoidance of denial.
   d. Interview the accused only.

180. When must the EEO-1 report be filed?
   a. Bi-annually, September 30.
   b. Annually, September 30.
   c. Annually, October 30.
   d. Bi-annually, October 30.

181. Risk assessment primarily analyses which of the following?
   a. The cost of business operations.
   b. The risk location.
   c. The risk impact to business continuity.

d. All of the above.

182. Anna is a teacher and advocates for pay equity and minimizing of pay disparity between jobs traditionally held by women and jobs traditionally held by men that have similar responsibilities. Anna is advocating for which of these concepts?
   a. Composite equity.
   b. Comparable worth.
   c. Pay adjustments.
   d. Pay review.

183. The ADA protects which of the following;
   a. Employees who acknowledge disabilities.
   b. Employees who are perceived to be disabled by employers.
   c. A and B.
   d. A only.

184. The Economic Growth and Tax Relief Reconciliation Act (EGTRRA) made a number of changes to existing limits, including the allowance for older workers to catch up on their retirement savings . These catch-up contributions are for employees of the age ---- and older.
   a. 50.
   b. 60.
   c. 40.
   d. 65.

185. The DEA company has refused the request of an employee requesting for an accommodation at the first instance by writing. The DEA company faces a potential ADA risk in which of the following areas;
   a. Refusing to provide an accommodation.
   b. Refusing to engage in an interactive process to search for a reasonable accommodation.
   c. Refusing to acknowledge the employee's disability.
   d. None of the above.

186. Wage compression refers to which of the following;
   a. Pay that is above the green circle.
   b. Higher wages offered to new workers than those that are given to existing workers.
   c. Pay practices that are illegal.
   d. Pay ranges that are based on internal equity with benchmarked positions.

187. An organisation that refuses to accommodate employee family/personal life concerns might face which of these risks;
   a. Reduced productivity.
   b. Higher recruitment costs.
   c. Increased absenteeism.

d. All of the above.

188. At an HR seminar, the speaker says, "green circles are dangerous and red circles are expensive". What are green circles and red circles?
   a. Green circles are employees who are paid below the minimum of the pay range for their jobs while Red circles are paid above the maximum pay range for their jobs.
   b. Green and red circles are functional payroll compressions.
   c. The speaker is referring to inverse discrimination in compensation.
   d. Green circles will create litigation problems for the red circles.

189. Compliance with the Sarbanes-Oxley Act for HR includes the following except?
   a. Reporting immediately substantial changes to the company's financial condition.
   b. Ensure that material liabilities from pending lawsuits are reported in financial statements.
   c. Investigation of disparate treatment of male caregivers.
   d. Non-retaliation against whistleblowers.

190. The Omnibus Budget Reconciliation Act of 1993 stipulates the following except?
   a. Tax deductions for executive pay be capped at $1,000,000 per year.
   b. Group health coverage be offered for children placed for adoption before the adoption is final.
   c. Group health plans honor qualified medical child-support orders.
   d. Executive pay be taxed twice as much as the minorities employed.

191. What is the formula for compa-ratio?
   a. Base salary*Midpoint progression.
   b. Base pay/Midpoint of salary range x 100.
   c. Compa-ratio has no formula, it is determined by benchmarking.
   d. Base pay/Benchmark job x 100.

192. The federal hourly minimum wage in 2015 is set at what amount?
   a. $8.25.
   b. $7.50.
   c. $7.35.
   d. $7.25.

193. Which of the following is not true about competency-based compensation?
   a. The greater the level of competence, the higher level of pay is available.
   b. It is a traditional pay structure.
   c. Competency profiles replace job descriptions.
   d. It places the responsibility of advancement on each employee.

194. What is the preferred way to determine employment eligibility?
   a. The form I-9.

b. <u>E-Verify.</u>
  c. USCIS database.
  d. Social Security Administration Internet Records.

195. Which of these is true about Social Security?
  a. Employers only deduct but do not contribute to social security payments.
  b. <u>Both employers and employees equally share payment of the 12.4% social security tax.</u>
  c. Social security is the same as Medicare payments.
  d. Both employers and employees equally share payment of the 2.9% social security tax.

196. A form of union security agreement where the employer may hire union or non-union workers but the non-union workers must pay a fee to cover collective bargaining costs is called;
  a. <u>Agency shop.</u>
  b. Union shop.
  c. Collective shop.
  d. Closed shop.

197. Employers have the responsibility to ensure the following except;
  a. Provide safe working environments.
  b. Pay wages for all work done by employees.
  c. <u>Engage only in constructive discharge.</u>
  d. Reimburse employees for expenses incurred on behalf of the employer.

198. Which of these is accurate about Compensatory time off?
  a. <u>Only public employers may compensate employees with comp time instead of overtime payments.</u>
  b. Both private & public employers may compensate employees with comp time.
  c. Only overtime pay applies to public employees, private employees can receive comp time.
  d. None of the above is accurate.

199. The following is true about Title IX except?
  a. It requires gender equity for boys and girls in every educational program that receives federal funding.
  b. It prohibits discrimination in sexual harassment or based on pregnancy.
  c. It addresses discrimination based on equal opportunity in athletics.
  d. <u>Title IX doesn't exist.</u>

200. A legal doctrine which states that, in many circumstances, an employer is responsible for the actions of employees performed within the course of their employment is called
  a. Statutory exceptions.
  b. <u>Respondeat superior.</u>
  c. Constructive responsibility.

d. Judicial precedent.

201. State unemployment insurance tax rate changes are based on which of the following?
    a. Compliance with the Federal Insurance Contribution Act (FICA).
    b. <u>On the number of employees terminated during the year</u>.
    c. Designation of FMLA leave.
    d. FLSA overtime and minimum wage dictates.

201. Common law doctrines are legal decisions made by judges over centuries. Which of the following is NOT a common law doctrine relevant to HR?
    a. Employment at will.
    b. Constructive discharge.
    c. <u>Arbitration.</u>
    d. Respondeat superior.

202. Which of the following is NOT true about FUTA tax rate?
    a. FUTA means Federal Unemployment Tax Act.
    b. <u>The FUTA tax rate in 2016 is 6% on organisational profit earned.</u>
    c. The FUTA tax rate is 6.0%, but includes a credit of 5.4% for timely payment of state UI taxes, making the effective FUTA tax rate 0.6 %.
    d. Employers who paid wages of $1,500 in any calendar quarter are subject to FUTA.

203. Why do organisations develop budgets?
    a. To ensure corporate goals are aligned with ecological realities.
    b. <u>To determine how much cash is required to achieve a goal.</u>
    c. To reduce the possibilities of fraud.
    d. To activate strategic planning.

204. Unemployment compensation is typically paid for a maximum of how many weeks within which the recipient must be pursuing employment?
    a. 20 weeks.
    b. 15 weeks.
    c. 25 weeks.
    d. <u>26 weeks.</u>

205. Tom claims his company fired him because he didn't commit perjury on the employer's behalf. Under which of these employment at will exceptions does Tom have a legal case?
    a. Contract Exception.
    b. <u>Public policy Exception.</u>
    c. Fraudulent misrepresentation.
    d. Duty of good faith and fair dealing.

206. How can employers reduce State Unemployment Insurance (SUI)?

a. Contesting ineligible unemployment claims.
b. Effective performance management process.
c. Employee termination must be for just cause with appropriate documentation.
d. All of the above.

207. The following are accurate about a SMART goal except;
a. Measurable.
b. Specific.
c. Response.
d. Action-oriented.

208. Which of the following voluntary benefits explanations is inaccurate?
a. Nonqualified plan - A plan that is nonforfeitable and receives favourable tax advantages.
b. Defined benefit-a pension plan where the employer provides a specific benefit upon retirement.
c. Defined contribution-The amount of contribution is known but the benefit paid is dependent on investment returns.
d. Qualified plan-A plan that meets ERISA requirements, provides tax advantages and all employees are eligible for.

209. The public policy exception of the employment-at-will doctrine can be applied in which of the following areas except;
a. Employees who engage in promissory estoppel.
b. Employees who refuse to break the law.
c. Employees who are whistleblowers.
d. Employees cooperating in a government investigation of employer wrongdoing.

210. The Employee Retirement Income Security Act of 1974 (ERISA) requires organizations to file three types of reports. Which of the following is NOT one of the reports;
a. Summary Plan Description.
b. Annual report.
c. Participant Benefit Rights Reports.
d. Health Portability Report.

211. All these are true about employment eligibility requirements except;
a. Newly hired employees must complete and sign section 1 of Form I-9 no later than the first day of employment.
b. Only private employers will be fined if the form I-9 is not completed.
c. Employers are responsible for completing and retaining the Form I-9.
d. Employers must complete this form to document verification of the employment eligibility of each new employee.

212. Tony has proved that his employer spread communication that damaged his reputation and was deliberately malicious. Tony can sue his employer under which of the following;
   a. **Defamation.**
   b. Constructive discharge.
   c. Harassment.
   d. Undue damages.

213. The Act which prohibits discrimination on the basis of health status, safeguards medical information and limits health insurance restrictions for preexisting conditions is called;
   a. OBRA.
   b. **HIPAA.**
   c. PPA.
   d. REA.

214. Gregg tells his subordinate that if she has sexual relations with him, she will get the promotion currently being offered. What form of sexual harassment is this?
   a. Hostile.
   b. **Quid pro quo.**
   c. Enticement.
   d. Sexual favors.

215. All these are true about a compressed work schedule except;
   a. A compressed work schedule allows an employee to work the traditional 40 hour week in less than the traditional workdays.
   b. **Compressed work schedules are only applicable to organisations with 25 or more employees.**
   c. An example is when a full-time employee scheduled for 40 hours works for four 10-hour days instead of five 8-hour days.
   d. Compressed work schedule is a form of positive employee relations strategy.

216. The Family Medical Leave Act (FMLA) of 1993 provides the following benefits except;
   a. 12 weeks of unpaid leave within a 12 month period.
   b. 26 weeks of unpaid leave for military caregiver leave.
   c. Reinstatement to the same/equivalent position at the end of leave.
   d. **Only jobs of comparable worth are eligible for FMLA.**

217. Which of these is true about a hostile work environment?
   a. Sexual favors that consensual.
   b. When an employer is not aware of harassment done by its managers.
   c. **A victim can be someone affected by unwelcome offensive conduct towards someone other than themselves.**
   d. Constructive recharge.

218. Which of the following employer category is not covered by the FMLA ?
   a. Private employers with 50+ employees.
   b. Worksites within a 75-mile radius.
   c. All private and public employers.
   d. A and B only.

219. Vestibule training can be defined as ;
   a. E-learning.
   b. Pre-learning.
   c. On-The-Job Training.
   d. Expert forecast.

220. Employees are eligible for FMLA under the following except;
   a. Employee must be in a union shop clause.
   b. Employee must have been employed for 12 months.
   c. Employee must work for an employer subject to FMLA.
   d. Employee must have worked for 1,250 hours during the 12 months preceding the leave.

221. Which of the following cases on sexual harassment did the Court reject the idea that "a mere existence of a grievance procedure and a policy against discrimination is enough to protect an employer from the acts of its supervisors" ?
   a. Harris v. Forklift Systems. 1993.
   b. Meritor Savings Bank v. Vinson. 1986.
   c. Faragher v. City of Boca Raton. 1998
   d. Burlington Industries v. Ellerth. 1998.

222. Under the FMLA, key employees may be denied reinstatement to their previous position if reinstatement would cause "substantial and grievous economic injury". Who is a key employee?
   a. Among the highest paid 10% of employees.
   b. A management staff.
   c. An executive.
   d. Top 5 performing staff.

223. These are components of an Affirmative Action Plan except;
   a. Organizational profile
   b. Placement of Incumbents in job groups
   c. Sample information from OFCCP.
   d. Comparison of Incumbency to Availability

224. Under the employee notice requirement of the FMLA, employees are required to do which of the following?
   a. Notify employer at least 30 days prior to expected start date of leave.
   b. In unplanned circumstances, notify employer as soon as practicable.

c. Notify employer retroactively.
d. <u>A and B.</u>

225. An employer is subject to vicarious liability to a victimized employee for the hostile actions created by a supervisor. What is vicarious liability?
   a. <u>An employer can be held accountable for the harmful actions of its employees, even if the employer is not aware of the action.</u>
   b. An employee is responsible for their actions.
   c. Vicarious liability means the same as constructive discharge.
   d. A legal term not relevant to HR discourse.

226. Which of the following FMLA Medical Certification forms provided by the DOL is for "serious injury or illness to covered service member"?
   a. WH-380-E.
   b. WH-380-F.
   c. WH-384.
   d. <u>WH-385.</u>

227. A forecasting and decision-making activity that relies on a group of experts to reach a consensus is called;
   a. <u>Delphi technique.</u>
   b. Competence training.
   c. Skill intervention.
   d. Synchronous training.

228. Which of these explanations of the types of FMLA is inaccurate?
   a. Continuous FMLA Leave - the employee is absent for an extended period of time.
   b. <u>Extended FMLA Leave - the employee's leave of 12 weeks is extended to 26 weeks.</u>
   c. Reduced FMLA Leave - the employee's regular schedule is reduced for a timeframe.
   d. Intermittent FMLA Leave - the employee is absent from work for multiple periods of time.

229. An employer can clearly express its prohibition of harassment by the following except;
   a. Develop anti-harassment policies and complaint procedures.
   b. <u>Leave investigation of allegations to the SEC.</u>
   c. Clearly express unacceptable conducts.
   d. Provide multiple avenues for reporting harassment.

230. Under the FMLA, what does a rolling 12-month period mean?
   a. <u>12 month period calculated retroactively from the date of the FMLA leave.</u>
   b. The calendar year.
   c. Any fixed 12-month period.
   d. The 12 month period when the leave begins.

231. A legal standard of care and professionalism is a component of;
    a. <u>Fiduciary responsibility.</u>
    b. Conflict of interest.
    c. Code of ethics.
    d. Executive orders

232. Workers' compensation require employers to assume responsibility for employees' injuries, illnesses and deaths related to employment. Some benefits covered are the following except;
    a. Medical and rehabilitation expenses.
    b. Income replacement during periods of disability.
    c. <u>Benefits to survivors of earthquakes.</u>
    d. Benefits to survivors in the event of an employee's death.

233. The Glass Ceiling Act of 1991 identified three barriers that prevented women and minorities from advancing to senior levels. Which of the following is not one of them?
    a. Societal Barriers.
    b. <u>Economical Barriers.</u>
    c. Internal structural Barriers.
    d. Governmental Barriers.

234. Which of the following is NOT a type of healthcare plan?
    a. Preferred Provider Organization (PPO).
    b. Point of Service (POS) plan.
    c. <u>Target Benefit plan.</u>
    d. Fee-for-Service (FFS) plan.

235. All these are human process interventions except;
    a. Conflict management
    b. <u>Total Quality Management.</u>
    c. Emotional Intelligence.
    d. Team building.

236. Which of these is not correct about USERRA provisions on reemployment reporting times?
    a. For a length of service of 1-30 days, the reporting time is the 1st scheduled full workday.
    b. For a length of service of 31-180 days; submit reemployment application no later than 14 days after end of service.
    c. For a length of service of 180 days or more; submit reemployment application no later than 90 days after end of service.
    d. <u>The reemployment reporting times do not apply to disabilities incurred during military service.</u>

237. The following are true about HR Development except;
    a. Reengineering realigns operations to add value to the customer.

b. Restructuring reduces redundancy to manage costs.
c. <u>Divestitures usually results in picketing.</u>
d. Outsourcing results in employees being acquired by an outsource provider.

238. USERRA provides that employers provide a leave of absence of up to 5 years for reservists called to active duty. Which of the following is true as well on USERRA provisions?
   a. Employers are not required to pay employees during military absences.
   b. Employee pension rights are protected during their absence.
   c. Employers must promptly reinstate regular employees to positions they will have earned if they remained on the job.
   d. <u>All of the above.</u>

239. A performance appraisal method that gives the employee the chance to share their performance perspective is called?
   a. Supervisory audit.
   b. Self-analysis.
   c. <u>360-degree assessment.</u>
   d. Peer review.

240. Which of these is true about continued employment under USERRA?
   a. Continued employment is not required under USERRA.
   b. Employees returning from a leave of 30 days but less than 181 days may not be discharged without cause for 6 months after reemployment.
   c. Employees returning from a leave of 181 days or more may not be discharged without cause for 1 year after reemployment.
   d. <u>B and C.</u>

241. Organizations have three main options to locate top talent except;
   a. Internal talent.
   b. <u>Internet blogs.</u>
   c. External talent.
   d. Alternative staffing methods

242. Employees have which of the following duties under the common law doctrine?
   a. Duty of loyalty.
   b. Duty of obedience.
   c. Duty of diligence.
   d. <u>All of the above.</u>

243. The following are human resource interventions except;
   a. <u>Management by Objectives.</u>
   b. Compensation.
   c. Diversity programs.

d. Performance management.

244. The CEO of GRET company has lunch with various employee levels at a cafe to discuss the company's goals and provide an avenue for answering questions. This is known as;
   a. Open lunches.
   b. <u>Brown-bag lunches.</u>
   c. Word of Mouth.
   d. Staff Cafes.

245. A safety management plan need not include;
   a. Ongoing worksite analysis.
   b. Senior management support.
   c. <u>Consistent OSHA inspections.</u>
   d. Fire prevention program.

246. The TEN Company determines employee engagement by getting the manager's manager to interview employees to provide insight into employee goals and satisfaction. This is called;
   a. Management by Walking Around.
   b. Employee focus.
   c. Managerial interview.
   d. <u>Skip-level interview.</u>

247. The following are techno-structural interventions except;
   a. <u>Fiduciary Responsibility.</u>
   b. Six Sigma.
   c. High-Involvement organizations.
   d. Total Quality Management.

248. Which of the explanations of the following Work/Life Balance programs is inaccurate?
   a. Telecommuting -working from home.
   b. Flextime -setting hours for which employees can handle their personal business.
   c. <u>Compressed Workweeks -Preventing overtime requirements for employee rest.</u>
   d. Job-sharing -where two part-time employees share one job.

249. A major disadvantage of sourcing internal talent only is;
   a. <u>A myopic view of the industry.</u>
   b. Diversity of the workforce.
   c. Increased training costs.
   d. Political competition.

250. Temi has requested that a union representative be at her disciplinary hearing as detailed under Weingarten rights. Temi's employer has three options, which of the following is not one of them?

a. Discontinue the interview until the union representative arrives.
b. Decide not to conduct the interview at all.
c. <u>Continue the interview and make a disciplinary decision according to NLRB standards.</u>
d. Give the employee the choice of voluntarily waiving the Weingarten rights and continuing the interview.

251. When an employee resigns because of a hostile boss who undermines him/her in front of colleagues, the employee can take legal action based on;
   a. Constructive allegations.
   b. <u>Constructive discharge.</u>
   c. Fair workplace doctrine.
   d. Promissory estoppel.

252. The following are workplace behavior issues except;
   a. Absenteeism.
   b. Dress code violations.
   c. Insubordination.
   d. <u>Resolutions.</u>

253. In a bid to determine the jobs necessary to realize corporate goals, HR must do the following except;
   a. <u>Determine the organization's key competition.</u>
   b. Assess the KSAs available within the organization.
   c. Determine the KSAs needed to attain the future goals.
   d. Conduct a gap analysis.

254. Which of the following is not a form of alternative dispute resolution;
   a. Constructive confrontation.
   b. <u>Verbal warning.</u>
   c. Arbitration.
   d. Mediation.

255. When an employer shares a building with another employer that is being picketed, which of these is NOT true?
   a. This kind of picketing is called Common Situs picketing.
   b. <u>This kind of picketing is called Recognitional Picketing.</u>
   c. The union engaged in picketing must ensure the picket signs clearly state the name of the employer being picketed.
   d. Restrict picketing to the entrance of the employer being picketed.

256. The following are true about these alternative staffing methods except;
   a. A Professional Employer Organization (PEO) becomes the employer of record.
   b. Outsourcing moves an entire function out to be handled by another company.

c. Job-sharing means two part-time employees join the PEO.
   d. None of the above.

257. Which of these is a lawful labour action?
   a. Work slowdown.
   b. Directed election.
   c. Secondary boycotts.
   d. Hot-cargo picketing.

258. Arbitration helps to resolve conflicts without lawsuit expenses. Which of the following is true about arbitration?
   a. Compulsory arbitration can be a contract requirement or mandated by a court system.
   b. A tripartite arbitration panel consists of 3 arbitrators who reach a joint decision.
   c. Binding arbitration is when parties accept that the arbitrator's decision is final.
   d. All of the above.

259. The following are from the four steps of risk management process except;
   a. Identify risks.
   b. Assess/analyze risks.
   c. Eliminate risks.
   d. Review/monitor risks.

260. Which of the following is true about temporary workers being unionized?
   a. Temporary employees who work side by side and have a community of interest with regular employees may be part of the bargaining unit.
   b. Temporary employees cannot be unionized as indicated in the Sturgis case.
   c. Temporary employees can be unionized but only if they have worked with the company for a duration of at least 12 months.
   d. None of the above.

261. When a salesperson's salary has a percentage dependent on his ability to sell company product or services, this percentage is known as;
   a. Bonus.
   b. Base pay.
   c. Commission.
   d. Incentives.

262. When picketing is done to advise consumers that goods have been produced by a company whose workers are on strike, this is called;
   a. Informational picketing.
   b. Consumer picketing.
   c. ULP picketing.
   d. Straight-line picketing.

263. Which of the following is the most effective way for management to avoid unionization of the workplace?
   a. Treat employees fairly.
   b. Give employees a voice in decisions that affect their work.
   c. All of the above.
   d. None of the above.

264. Management may do which of the following during a union campaign?
   a. State the consequences of unionization based on past facts.
   b. Conduct campaign activities around the polling area.
   c. Promise benefits to employees in the bargaining unit.
   d. None of the above.

265. Workers Compensation covers the following except:
   a. Immediate injuries that occur at the workplace.
   b. Injuries that occur while telecommuting.
   c. Injuries developed because of workplace conditions.
   d. Injuries that occur while attending a work-related function.

266. Which of the following is a NOT measurable indicator of employee satisfaction?
   a. Absenteeism.
   b. Complaints against managers.
   c. Turnover.
   d. Employee surveys.

267. A defined contribution plan relies on fixed contributions from employees and employers. Which of the following types of defined contribution plans is inaccurately explained?
   a. Profit-sharing plan - the maximum contribution is the lesser of $50,000 or 25% of compensation.
   b. 401(k) plan - the plan must not provide greater benefits to highly compensated employees.
   c. Money Purchase plan - the percentage of employee contribution is varied and not fixed.
   d. Target Benefit plan - Formulas are used to calculate the contribution needed to reach a predetermined benefit amount at retirement.

268. How many weeks of leave is required for caring for a military family member who is sick or injured under the FMLA ?
   a. 12.
   b. 26.
   c. 38.
   d. 20.

269. A major feature of an independent contractor are all these except;
   a. No control or direction of tasks completed by the worker.
   b. Minimal stock investment made into the business.
   c. A specific period for the relationship.
   d. No existence of benefits.

270. The FMLA requires that 12 weeks of leave be given for the following except?
   a. When a party of interest is involved with the NLRB.
   b. Serious health condition for the employee.
   c. Childbirth and caring for a child under one year old.
   d. Caring for a child, spouse or parent with a serious health condition.

271. An indirect veto of a legislative bill by the president or a governor by retaining the bill unsigned until it is too late for it to be dealt with during the legislative session is called;
   a. Perfect veto.
   b. Presidential veto.
   c. Quorum veto.
   d. Pocket veto.

272. The legal doctrine which states that a promise is enforceable by law when the promisor makes a promise to the promisee who relies on it to his or her own detriment is called?
   a. Vestibule promissory.
   b. Promissory estoppel.
   c. Fiduciary standard.
   d. Respondeat superior.

273. A labour market analysis will look at the following except;
   a. Unemployment rate.
   b. New and old competition.
   c. Geographic labor availability.
   d. Workforce plan.

274. Nonqualified Deferred compensation plans are available only to a limited number of employees at the executive level. Which of the following is NOT true about Nonqualified Deferred Compensation plans?
   a. The plans allow employees to defer income in excess of limits placed on qualified plans.
   b. The plans are protected by ERISA or subject to ERISA testing requirements.
   c. Rabbi Trusts provide retirement income that are unsecure and subject to creditor claims.
   d. Excess deferral plan is an example of a nonqualified deferred compensation plan.

275. A form of training where real world scenarios are used to train participants is called;
   a. On the job training.
   b. Plateau analysis.

c. Case study.
d. Banquet training.

276. Non-monetary benefits offered to employees in lieu of services provided by them to the organization is called;
   a. Affirmative action.
   b. Indirect compensation.
   c. Variable pay.
   d. Bonuses.

277. A skill inventory is useful for the following except;
   a. To help determine poor-performing employees.
   b. To help organizations assess their ability to meet company goals.
   c. Understanding the current skills available to aid strategic planning.
   d. It helps to understand the future skill requirements.

278. Salting can be described as;
   a. When workers deliberately work slower than they usually do.
   b. When the union hires someone to get a job in a company and help organize the company.
   c. When the union engages in subtle strikes against the company.
   d. When the union hires a recognized picketer to picket the company.

279. The following are examples of indirect compensation except;
   a. Leave policy.
   b. Retirement benefits.
   c. Pay for performance.
   d. Home insurance.

280. Rachel heard via the grapevine that her boss will be moving away to another country. She promptly spoke with the HR Manager about her interest in the potential opening. Rachel has engaged in which of the following;
   a. Ambitious Request.
   b. Job bidding.
   c. Job posting.
   d. Insubordination.

290. The following are comparative forms of performance review except;
   a. Field review.
   b. Ranking.
   c. Forced ranking.
   d. Paired comparison

300. The following risk management tools are legal requirements except?
   a. EEO-1 forms.
   b. Employee handbooks.
   c. Affirmative Action plans.
   d. FMLA documentation.

301. Ann is a top performer in her department, she is not motivated by pay or compliments from her boss, Ann has the personal motivation of working smart for her own satisfaction and values challenging work. This is an example of;
   a. Personal fulfilment.
   b. Personal ambition.
   c. Intrinsic reward.
   d. Individual productivity.

302. The ZYX company has a diverse workforce and recently implemented a succession plan. The following are envisaged HR challenges to this new implementation except;
   a. Virtual interviewing.
   b. Poor communication.
   c. Perceived indiscriminate promotions.
   d. Senior staff with obsolete skills in the succession plan.

303. Which of the following is true about the Critical Incident performance review?
   a. Employees are listed from the highest to the lowest performer.
   b. Numeric rating scales are made for all employees.
   c. Supervisors make notes of particular good or bad performance issues and present these during the review.
   d. Job descriptions are used to create dimensions to state the key requirements of the job.

304. When all employees are reviewed at the same time during a review period, this is known as;
   a. Bi-annual review period
   b. Focal review period.
   c. Joint review period.
   d. Team review period.

305. Under ERISA of 1974, what does a Summary Plan Description mean?
   a. A description of employees under the Affirmative Action Plan.
   b. Information about the FMLA and FLSA standards.
   c. Information about a benefit plan, including provisions, policies and eligibility requirements.
   d. An annual report to be filed on all employee benefit plans.

306. Which of these is true about the Fair Labor Standard Act (FLSA)?

a. It negates the employment at will.
b. <u>Short breaks less than 20 minutes are compensable.</u>
c. Overtime requires the zero-based budgeting.
d. All employees in the middle management are non-exempt.

307. Which of the following is NOT true under employee participation requirements in ERISA?
a. Eligibility requires completion of one year of service or an employee that has reached the age of 21.
b. Employees may not be excluded from the plan on the basis of age.
c. Eligible employees must become plan participants no later than the first day of the plan year.
d. <u>The employee becomes vested 100% after a year.</u>

308. Adverse impact can be determined if;
a. 80% of the selection rate of a group of men is higher than 80% of the selection rate of women.
b. <u>80% of the selection rate of a group is higher than the percentage of the selection rate of a protected group.</u>
c. % of the highest rate is greater than the mode selection rate of the women in the group.
d. Black people are given more roles to balance the diversity of the workforce for the OFCCP.

309. What does vesting mean?
a. <u>When employees own employer contributions to their pension plan.</u>
b. When employers distribute pension contributions.
c. Qualified domestic relations orders.
d. When employers determine benefit entitlements.

310. An organization where knowledge is originated, obtained and disseminated freely to enable the company compete effectively is called?
a. Strategic organization.
b. Techno-structural organization.
c. <u>Learning organization.</u>
d. Systematic organization.

311. Which of the following statements about vesting is NOT true?
a. Cliff vesting is when participants become 100% vested after a specified period of time not exceeding 5 years.
b. <u>Employees are not 100% vested in their own money.</u>
c. Immediate vesting is when employees are 100% vested as soon as they meet the eligibility requirements.
d. Graded vesting must allow for 20% vesting after 3 years and full vesting after 7 years of service.

312. Which act requires that federal contractors with contracts of $25,000 or more list job openings with state employment agencies?
   a. VEVRAA.
   b. OFCCP.
   c. EEOC.
   d. HIPAA.

313. What are the key requirements of the Retirement Equity Act (REA) of 1984?
   a. Lowered age limits for participation and vesting in pension plans.
   b. Required written approval from spouse if participant refused survivor benefits.
   c. None of the above.
   d. A and B only.

314. The Uniform Guidelines on Employee Selection Procedures (UGESP) states that;
   a. Any selection tool must be reviewed by the EEOC.
   b. Any selection tool that has an adverse impact should be expunged.
   c. Any selection tool should be job-related and a valid predictor of job success.
   d. Any selection tool that requires a college degree be reviewed.

315. Key provisions of the Older Worker Benefit Protection Act (OWBPA) of 1990 include the following except?
   a. Individual employees must be given 21 days to consider waiver agreements before they are required to sign.
   b. Employees in a group which are 40 or older must be given 45 days to consider waiver agreements.
   c. Employees may revoke signed agreements within 7 days.
   d. The federal agency for enforcement of the OWBPA is the DOL.

316. A violation in which the employer either knowingly failed to comply with a legal requirement or acted with plain indifference to employee safety is called;
   a. Maximus violation.
   b. Serious violation.
   c. Willful violation.
   d. Direct violation.

317. The Act that allows for catch-up contributions for employees older than 50 years of age is called?
   a. Older Worker Benefit Protection Act of 1990.
   b. Omnibus Budget Reconciliation Act of 1993.
   c. Economic Growth and Tax Relief Reconciliation Act of 2001.
   d. Unemployment Compensation Amendments of 1992.

318. An example of a tactical accountability measure on employee relations is?
   a. Workplace violence.
   b. Number of claims filed with the EEOC.
   c. Employee complaints.
   d. Team spirit in the organisation.

319. Which of the following is a key focus of the Pension Protection Act (PPA) of 2006?
   a. For employers to fully fund pension plans to avoid future cash shortfalls.
   b. To legalize pension plans for employees over the age of 70.
   c. For employees to contribute equal percentages to benefit plans.
   d. None of the above.

320. An OSHA violation that has a direct relationship to job safety and health but is not serious in nature is classified as;
   a. Mild violation.
   b. Other-than-serious violation.
   c. Permit violation.
   d. De-minimis violation.

321. Companies usually outsource specialized functions at what stage?
   a. Decline.
   b. Maturity.
   c. Development.
   d. Startup.

322. The BTQ company application form for recruiters gives higher scores to some aspects of the job. This is a ;
   a. Weighted employment application
   b. Biased employment application
   c. Job-specific employment application
   d. Internal screening employment application.

323. Which of the following is NOT a characteristic of a corporation?
   a. Liability is limited to assets owned by the corporation.
   b. Ownership cannot be transferred freely by sales of stock.
   c. There is a central management structure.
   d. The life of the corporation can extend beyond the life of the founder.

324. The RST company always uses at least 4 interviewers and leaves the candidates to guide the interview. This is an example of;
   a. Stress interview.
   b. Panel interview.
   c. Non-directive interview.

d. B & C.

325. How can HR determine if an injury is work-related or not?
   a. Injuries from a voluntary wellness activity is not work-related.
   b. Injuries from food prepared for personal consumption is not work-related.
   c. Common cold/flu ailments are not work-related.
   d. All of the above.

326. Ken interviewed ten candidates and rates them all the same. This form of interviewer bias is;
   a. Cultural Noise
   b. Leniency
   c. Stereotyping
   d. Average/Central Tendency.

327. Why should injuries be analysed to determine if they are work-related or not?
   a. To avoid litigation costs.
   b. To ensure documentation of all employee communicable diseases.
   c. To determine OSHA recordability and compensability under Workers' Compensation.
   d. For voluntary safety analysis.

328. Bambi noticed that Sophia, a candidate scored particularly low on the well-trusted company test and because of this, she did not bother to listen to Sophia during the interview. This is;
   a. Nonverbal Bias.
   b. Horn Effect.
   c. Knowledge of Predictor.
   d. Harshness Effect

329. Which of the following are exceptions to the employment-at-will doctrine?
   a. Promissory estoppels.
   b. Duty of good faith and fair dealing.
   c. Employment contract.
   d. All of the above.

330. Bob, the HR Manager of Gingle Inc. has decided to utilize the Cognitive Ability Test (CAT) for the company's candidates. He tells management that the test is reliable and valid. What does he mean?
   a. Reliable means the test produces consistent results over time; Valid means the test has construct criterion.
   b. Valid means the test enhances the employment decision while Reliable means the tests can be trusted.

    c. <u>Reliable means the test produces consistent results over time, Valid means the test accurately measures the desired characteristics.</u>
    d. Valid means it has the right content, construct and criteria, Reliable means UGESP compliant.

331. Which of these benefits is inaccurately explained?
    a. Accidental Death and Dismemberment (AD&D) Insurance - provides insurance in the event of a death of a covered person or the loss of a bodily function.
    b. <u>A cash-balance plan is not a defined-benefit plan.</u>
    c. Money purchase plan - a type of defined-contribution plan that is similar to a profit-sharing plan, except that the contribution amounts are fixed.
    d. 401(k) plans, 403(b)plans (for nonprofit workers) and 457 plans (for public employees) are defined contribution plans.

332. Ann has a presentation on test validity to a group of HR professionals. Which of the information on her slide is incorrect?
    a. Content validity is when a driving test is administered to a delivery person who drives 90% of the time on the job.
    b. Construct validity is when a test measures candidate characteristics and successful performance on the job.
    c. <u>Criterion Validity is not predictive in nature.</u>
    d. The content validity is more legally defensible than the construct validity.

333. Using a competency model, assessing&developing leadership capabilities and monitoring/measuring talent management are elements of which of the following;
    a. Organization development.
    b. <u>Talent Management.</u>
    c. Talent portfolio.
    d. Staffing Strategy.

334. A candidate has a criminal record. What should HR not consider?
    a. How does the type of crime relate to the position applied for?
    b. How recent was the conviction?
    c. <u>What is the level of embarrassment to the company?</u>
    d. What is the level of risk to customers, co-workers and others in the workplace?

335. An interest assessment means;
    a. <u>A tool used to understand the development opportunities that will engage top talent.</u>
    b. The staff indicates interest in a senior role via his/her supervisor.
    c. A tool used to determine the competences in the company's industry.
    d. A staffing strategy for organizations in the maturity stage.

336. The gathering of information about an employee's education, skills, development programs, training and samples of work in order to plan development opportunities is known as;
   a. Talent portfolio.
   b. <u>Career portfolio.</u>
   c. Strategic portfolio.
   d. KBI portfolio.

337. Company BTW is debating on the suitability of a candidate for the role of Chief Operating Officer. It has been determined that a consumer report will help make an informed decision. What is a consumer report?
   a. A report that the Fair Credit Reporting Act (FCRA) has expunged.
   b. A report that establishes the use of background investigations
   c. <u>A report containing information about an individual's character, reputation, lifestyle or credit history.</u>
   d. A report that the employee has no idea is being gathered about him.

338. Skill variety, task identity, task significance, autonomy and feedback are all forms of;
   a. Job Analysis.
   b. Needs assessment.
   c. Job responsibilities.
   d. <u>Job enrichment</u>.

339. Bill has sued company GTF for not following the FCRA regulations on obtaining a consumer report on him. What could company GTF have done to avoid this allegation?
   a. Disclosed to Bill that a consumer report will be obtained on him for employment purposes.
   b. Get written authorization from Bill to obtain the consumer report.
   c. Provide Bill with a copy of the report before taking an adverse action based on the report.
   d. <u>All of the above.</u>

340. The following are true about High Potential (HiPos) Employees except;
   a. HiPos are high potential employees identified as future organization leaders.
   b. Identifying HiPos is difficult because current performance may not predict future performance.
   c. <u>HiPos are useful in staffing risk assessment and mitigation.</u>
   d. The Myers-Briggs Type indicator can help evaluate potential HiPos.

341. A negligent-hiring lawsuit has been brought against the TYD Inc. What defense does the Inc. have?
   a. The Inc conducted reference checks with previous employers.
   b. The Inc conducted criminal record checks.
   c. The Inc verified all government-issued licenses.

d. <u>All of the above.</u>

342. What is a key difference between a mentor and a coach?
    a. <u>**Mentoring is based on an informal personal interest while a coach is involved at the organization's expense or prompting.**</u>
    b. A mentor is a counsellor while a coach is a developer.
    c. A coach focuses on career development while a mentor focuses on self-development.
    d. There is no key difference.

343. The Tank company has an embezzlement charge against it and has lost significant finances due to fraudulent discrepancies in its financial and audit departments. The CEO wants a polygraph test to be included in the investigations. As the HR Manager, what is your advice?
    a. The Employee Polygraph Protection Act (EPPA) prohibits private employers from using polygraph test in any circumstance.
    b. Only federal contractors with national defense, national security can use polygraph tests on employees.
    c. <u>**The CEO can use the polygraph tests but only in an ongoing investigation of an economic loss to the Tank company such as this.**</u>
    d. The polygraph test will result in lawsuits from the contentious employees in the financial and audit departments, it is better not used.

344. Of the following OSHA violation categories, which definition is inaccurate?
    a. Other than serious - could have a direct impact on the safety of employees.
    b. Serious - substantial probability of death or serious harm.
    c. <u>**De-minimus - Intentional violation of the OSH act.**</u>
    d. Failure to abate - Employer failed to abate a prior violation.

345. The following coaching sources are correct except;
    a. Internal sources.
    b. <u>**Parallel sources.**</u>
    c. External sources.
    d. Virtual sources.

346. The following are included in the strategy implementation stage except;
    a. Develop tactical goals.
    b. Develop budget.
    c. <u>**Environmental scan.**</u>
    d. Develop action plans.

347. Medical examinations are allowable, only when;
    a. The purpose is job-related and of business necessity.
    b. All applicants in the job category underwent the medical examination.
    c. The exam safeguards the workplace.

d. <u>A & B only.</u>

348. Which of the following is not true about OSHA recordkeeping requirements?
   a. Employers are to record health and safety incidents yearly.
   b. Employers are to document steps they took to comply with OSHA regulations.
   c. <u>Documented evidence of employee pay deductions pertaining to wilful injuries.</u>
   d. All of the above.

349. Training may take place on one of three levels except?
   a. <u>Instructional.</u>
   b. Individual.
   c. Task.
   d. Organizational.

350. The OSHA form used as the Log of Work-related Injuries and Illnesses is called;
   a. OSHA form 310.
   b. <u>OSHA form 300.</u>
   c. OSHA form 333.
   d. OSHA form 300A.

351. Drug screening tests are;
   a. Frowned upon by the EEOC.
   b. <u>Recommended by OSHA to reduce job-related accidents.</u>
   c. Against the ADA medical-examination requirements.
   d. Related to productivity and performance only.

352. The OSHA form 300A is used for which of the following?
   a. Employer violations.
   b. <u>Summary of Work-related Injuries and Illnesses.</u>
   c. Summary of Non-work related Injuries and Illnesses.
   d. This is not an OSHA form.

353. Which of these is inaccurate concerning governmental training funding?
   a. The Workforce Investment Act (WIA) backs the federal funding of training programs by state agencies.
   b. <u>For state training funds, it must be evident that the training program will add value to national concerns.</u>
   c. Some states use federal funding to reimburse training costs to employers.
   d. Employers must submit an application to be approved for participation and maintain accurate documentation to receive reimbursement.

354. The REW company has a total of 10 employees. Is the REW company required to complete and file OSHA forms?

a. Yes, all employers are required to abide by OSHA.
b. <u>No, only employers with 11 or more employees are required to file OSHA forms.</u>
c. Yes, employers with 10 or more employees are required to file OSHA forms.
d. No, the REW company has low injury rates due to few employees.

355. Which of the following is not an organizational structural change?
   a. Downsizing.
   b. Reengineering.
   c. <u>Employment contracts.</u>
   d. Mergers and Acquisitions.

356. TIm, the HR Manager of a company with a total of 21 employees has informed the CEO that the company does not need to fill out the OSHA form 300 (Log) and OSHA form 301 (Incident Report). Is Tim right?
   a. <u>Yes, only if a recordable work-related injury or illness has not occurred.</u>
   b. No, it is a requirement for the form 300 and 301 to be filled.
   c. Yes, companies with 21 employees are not required to fill the OSHA forms.
   d. None of the above.

357. Kinesthetic learning can be defined as?
   a. Virtual learning.
   b. Measurable learning.
   c. <u>Hands-on learning.</u>
   d. Objective learning.

358. Employers must fill out and post the OSHA form 300A (Summary) monthly, even if no recordable work-related injuries or illnesses occurred. What is wrong with this statement?
   a. <u>The form 300A is posted annually not monthly.</u>
   b. The employees fill the OSHA forms not the employers.
   c. If no injury occurred, no forms should be filed.
   d. The statement is accurate.

359. Which of these supersedes the employment at will doctrine ;
   a. Employment contracts.
   b. Public protest exception.
   c. Implied contract exception.
   d. <u>A&C.</u>

360. Which of these injuries is not work-related?
   a. An injured employee was present in the work place as a member of the general public at the time of injury.
   b. The illness is the common cold or flu.
   c. The injury is as a result of the employee preparing meals for personal consumption.

d. All of the above.

361. The learning curve of routine tasks such as operating a cash register is usually;
    a. Negatively Accelerating Learning Curve.
    b. Target Guided Learning Curve.
    c. Positively Accelerating Learning Curve.
    d. Plateau Learning Curve.

362. OSHA forms must be retained for how long following the end of the calendar year they cover?
    a. 10 years.
    b. 1 year.
    c. 5 years.
    d. 6 months.

363. The following are correct about employment contracts except;
    a. Usually reserved for senior-level managers, doctors and professors.
    b. Usually include the terms and conditions of employment.
    c. It is based on the employment at will doctrine.
    d. Usually require confidentiality of proprietary information.

364. When an employee who is the subject of the OSHA form 301 Incident Report requests for a copy, in what timeframe must the form 301 be provided to the employee?
    a. 7 calendar days.
    b. By the end of the next business day.
    c. 7 business days.
    d. 15 calendar days.

365. A learning curve that begins with a slow start in learning that increases as the learner understands the different aspects of the task is called;
    a. Positively Accelerating Learning Curve.
    b. Negatively Accelerating Learning Curve.
    c. S-shaped Learning Curve.
    d. Plateau Learning Curve.

366. The Act which requires that businesses with 20 or more employees provide health plan continuation coverage of up to 36 months for employees that leave/resign their jobs for qualifying events is called?
    a. HIPAA.
    b. COBRA.
    c. PPA.
    d. EGTRRA.

367. These are all true about the Immigration Reform and Control Act (IRCA) of 1986 except;
   a. Employers are required to complete the Form I-9 for all new hires within the first 3 days of employment.
   b. Employers are required to maintain I-9 files for 3 years from the date of hire or 1 year after the date of termination.
   c. Employers can use the E-Verify to comply with OSHA requirements.
   d. The IRCA addresses illegal immigration into the United States.

368. Employers may file a Notice of Contest within 15 days of an OSHA citation. What is a Notice of Contest?
   a. An objection to an unannounced OSHA inspection.
   b. An objection in writing to an OSHA citation or notice of proposed penalty.
   c. All of the above.
   d. None of the above.

369. Where a rapid increase in learning levels off and no additional progress occurs for an extended period of time is known as;
   a. S-shaped Learning Curve.
   b. Plateau Learning Curve.
   c. L-shaped Learning Curve.
   d. Negatively Accelerating Learning Curve.

370. Why are exit interviews necessary?
   a. It provides an opportunity to communicate why the employee is leaving.
   b. It helps to understand improvements the organisation could make to enhance retention.
   c. It opens the door for re-hiring if desirable.
   d. All of the above.

371. An interactive training method that provides the learner with an opportunity to try new skills or practice procedures in a setting that will not endanger the inexperienced trainee is called;
   a. Presentation.
   b. Simulation.
   c. Equipment Training.
   d. Socratic seminar.

372. The Worker Adjustment Retraining Notification (WARN) Act of 1988 requires that 60 days advance notice be given to either employees or their union representatives in the event of mass layoffs or plant closings. When is this not required;
   a. When the company is under the employment at will doctrine.
   b. When a natural disaster applied to the plant closing or mass layoff.
   c. The company is faltering and is seeking additional funding.
   d. B & C.

373. When inexperienced workers become familiar and gain experience using equipment that requires actual practice is known as;
   a. **Vestibule training.**
   b. Virtual training.
   c. Programmed instruction.
   d. Facilitation.

374. The following interview questions are lawful except?
   a. **Have you ever been arrested?**
   b. Is there anything that will prevent you from meeting work schedules?
   c. Are you 18 years or older?
   d. Are you authorized to work in the United States?

375. The following are experiential training methods (real-time situations) except?
   a. Demonstration.
   b. One-on-One.
   c. **Productivity.**
   d. Kinesthetic.

376. A layoff is taking place in DEW Company. As the HR Manager, what is your major consideration?
   a. Document the business reason clearly to prevent disparate impact allegations.
   b. Use objective and documented performance appraisals to remove low performers.
   c. **A & B.**
   d. Be the employee champion.

377. Which of the following is inaccurate about the following training delivery methods?
   a. Synchronous - Training occurring at the same time with the instructor.
   b. Asynchronous - Self-paced training.
   c. **Electronic Performance Support Systems (EPSS) - A form of classroom intervention.**
   d. Blended learning - Using multiple delivery methods.

378. The Workforce Investment Act helps with the following except;
   a. Provide job-training program to improve worker skills.
   b. **Balance workforce redundancy with retirement.**
   c. Reduce reliance on welfare.
   d. Improve workforce quality.

379. A training seating best suited for video presentations and lectures is known as;
   a. Banquet-style seating.
   b. Classroom-style seating.
   c. U-shaped style seating.
   d. **Theater-style seating.**

380. The eligibility requirements of the Trade Adjustment Assistance (TAA) of 2002 include the following except;
   a. <u>Workers must have submitted an individual petition to the EEOC and DOJ.</u>
   b. The workers must have been laid off or had their pay reduced by 20%.
   c. The employer's sales or production levels must have declined.
   d. The loss of jobs must be largely due to increased imports.

381. A training where participants will be taking part in small group discussions is best suited for which of the following seatings?
   a. Classroom style seating.
   b. U-shaped style seating.
   c. Chevron-style seating
   d. <u>Banquet-style seating.</u>

382. Which of these acronyms is expanded wrongly?
   a. FMLA-Family Medical Leave Act.
   b. NLRB-National Labour Relations Board.
   c. <u>COBRA-Consolidated Omnibus Budget Restitution Act.</u>
   d. VEVRAA-Vietnam Era Veterans Readjustment Act.

383. A training evaluation which occurs before the implementation of the training is called;
   a. Training evaluation.
   b. Reinforced evaluation.
   c. <u>Formative evaluation.</u>
   d. Summative evaluation.

384. The Techy multinational corporation prefers to fill management positions in its host countries with the best-qualified persons regardless of their country of origin. Instead, the Yelp multinational corporation fills its management positions with the Host-Country Nationals (HCNs). Which of the statements below is correct in light of the above?
   a. <u>Yelp uses a polycentric approach while Techy uses a geocentric approach.</u>
   b. Techy uses a regiocentric approach while Yelp uses a polycentric approach.
   c. Techy uses a geocentric approach while yelp uses an ethnocentric approach.
   d. Yelp uses the regiocentric approach while Techy uses the geocentric approach.

385. Which of the following is used to determine participant knowledge prior to the training design?
   a. Job analysis.
   b. Prior test.
   c. Pilot test.
   d. <u>Pre-test.</u>

386. Identify which of these is not a BFOQ?
   a. Mandatory retirement at a certain age for airline pilots.
   b. A religious school requires its principal or deans to be members of its religious sect.
   c. A black neighborhood store requires only African-Americans to apply.
   d. A therapy college invites application from all races and color.

387. A test which uses a focus group of participants to evaluate the relevance of the training content to the training objectives from which their feedback influences the final training delivery is called?
   a. Pilot test.
   b. Pre-test.
   c. Prime test.
   d. Post-test.

388. The balanced scorecard is a management tool that ties the outcome of each department together in one measurement system. Which of the following areas does the balanced scorecard NOT track information?
   a. Financial Results.
   b. Statutory protection.
   c. How employees are hired and trained to achieve organization goals.
   d. Customer results.

389. Under the ADEA, a waiver of rights is valid only when the protected employee has been given how many days to review the agreement?
   a. 21 days
   b. 49 days.
   c. 48 days.
   d. 45 days.

390. The following are true about the summative evaluation as developed by Donald Kirkpatrick except?
   a. Reaction - measures the initial reaction of the training participants.
   b. Learning - measures whether participants learned the information presented.
   c. Behavior - measures the participant behavior during the training.
   d. Results - measures if the training has an impact on business results.

391. Ann assaulted her boss because he looked at her the wrong way. It was investigated that Ann had anger management issues and has consistently physically assaulted all authority figures in her life. HR had no information on this because Ann was mild-mannered all through her interviews and a background check was considered unnecessary. This is an example of?
   a. Bias in recruitment
   b. The Halo effect.
   c. Negligent hiring.

d. A violation of the HRCI code for the HR department.

392. 360 degrees performance review can be described as which of the following;
    a. Performance review by everyone in the organization.
    b. Performance review by two or more supervisors.
    c. Performance feedback from not just the supervisors but coworkers, customers and subordinates.
    d. Performance review by oneself.

393. The electronic storage system must follow these instructions from the U.S. Citizen and Immigration Services;
    a. No unauthorized access.
    b. Ensure the integrity, accuracy and reliability of storage system.
    c. High degree of legibility and readability.
    d. All the above.

394. The following are true about comparison performance appraisal methods except;
    a. Ranking - employees are listed from the order of the highest to the lowest performer.
    b. Forced ranking-employees are ranked according to the bell curve.
    c. Rating scales-employees are rated according to a short performance essay.
    d. Paired comparison-all employees in the group are compared to one employee.

395. Ann created a literary piece for her organisation. On her resignation, she declared that she owns the copyright to this piece and any use of the piece by the company without her consent will be contested in court. Is Ann right?
    a. Ann is wrong, her employer owns the copyright.
    b. Ann is wrong, the literary piece can be used by either Ann or the company.
    c. Ann is right, she created the literary piece
    d. Ann is right, the Copyright Act of 1976 backs her declaration.

396. A management development program is best achieved by;
    a. Participative management styles.
    b. Exposure to financial and technology competences.
    c. Assigning a mentor or coach.
    d. Inspiring leadership traits by training.

397. The work for hire exception means;
    a. A musician employed by a recording agency owns the master rights but the recording agency owns the musical rights.
    b. A freelance author has been commissioned to create a book, the copyright of that book is owned by the freelance author.
    c. A freelance artist has been commissioned to create a work, the copyright of the artist's work is owned by the person who commissioned the work, not the artist.

d. A freelance author has been commissioned to create a book, the copyright of the book is owned by the author and the person who commissioned the book.

398. The following are Instructional Methods except;
    a. <u>Performance-based training methods.</u>
    b. Active training methods.
    c. Passive training methods.
    d. Experiential Training methods.

399. Which of the following is true about copyright laws?
    a. Copyrights protect original works for the lifetime of the author only.
    b. <u>Copyrights protect original works for the lifetime of the author plus 70 years.</u>
    c. Copyrights protect the original work of the company that employed the writer.
    d. Copyrights protect the latent work of the author for the lifetime of the author plus 70 years.

400. Which is not true about the following Training program delivery mechanisms?
    a. Electronic Performance Support Systems (EPSS)-A tool integrated in the computer system with instant information access.
    b. Programmed Instruction-Self-paced training.
    c. <u>Online Bulletin boards-blended learning.</u>
    d. Distance learning-virtual classroom.

401. Copyright laws for works-for-hire has the following protection;
    a. Protection for the shorter of 95 years from the first year of publication.
    b. Protection for 120 years from the year of creation.
    c. <u>A and B.</u>
    d. Protection for the 95 years and 120 years after the lifetime of the creator.

402. In which of these situations is the Chevron-style seating preferable?
    a. When training is being led by a facilitator not a lecturer.
    b. When participants are of equal status.
    c. For collaborative training.
    d. <u>For training where participants will be engaged in several activities.</u>

403. In what circumstance can copyrights be used without permission;
    a. Public domain.
    b. Fair use doctrine.
    c. Work for hire exception
    d. <u>A and B only.</u>

404. Which of these is true about the summative evaluation methods;
    a. Reaction - measures the initial reaction of the participants.

b. Behavior - measures whether new skills were successfully transferred to the job.
c. Results - measures if the training impacted business results.
d. All of the above.

405. The Fair Use doctrine states that the use of a work for the purpose of criticism, commentary or news reporting depends on these factors except;
a. The purpose and character of the use.
b. The nature of the copyright law to be focused on.
c. The amount of work to be used.
d. The effect the use of the material will have on the potential market value of the work.

406. Ken invented and patented a mini-flakes machine to transfer cornflakes from the pack to the bowl. This machine has been used by almost all homes that have kids from 2 - 7 years old. The following is true about Ken's patent except;
a. Ken's invention is protected by the design patents which is limited to 14 years.
b. Ken's invention is protected by utility patents which is limited to 20 years.
c. Ken's invention is protected by food patents which is limited for 14 years.
d. Ken's invention is protected by the plant patents which is limited to 20 years.

407. The method of examining your organization's technology, processes, structure and human resources, then developing action strategies to improve these is called;
a. Organisational Enhancement
b. Occupational Development.
c. Organisational Restructuring.
d. Organisational Development.

408. The HR Manager of GTH Inc. has decided that to motivate employees to perform at a high level of productivity, a job satisfaction survey will be done annually. Information from this survey will be used to finetune employee relations and benefits processes. The HR Manager has engaged in;
a. Organisational development.
b. Organisational Improvement.
c. Workforce motivation.
d. OD Interventions.

409. The four categories of interventions in Organisation Development (OD) by Cummings and Worley are;
a. Strategic, Cultural, Technological, Human Process
b. Strategic, Techno-structural, Human Process, Human Resource Management.
c. Strategic, Structural, Human Procedure, Human Resource Development
d. Strategic, Structural, Human Process, Human Resource Development.

410. Ann has been a HR professional in YTT Inc. for 5 years, she has been asked to give examples of strategic OD interventions to the newly employed HR management trainees. Which of these is correct;
   a. Strategic OD interventions is the task of management not HR.
   b. Change management, Knowledge management and Intervention management.
   c. Change management, knowledge management and Learning organizations.
   d. Change management, Communities of Practice and Knowledge management.

411. Kurt Lewin identified 3 stages of change. Which of these is incorrect?
   a. The three stages of change are unfreezing, moving and refreezing.
   b. Discipline and focus is most integral in the moving stage.
   c. The unfreezing stage communicates the need for change.
   d. The refreezing stage is when the new change becomes the norm.

412. Change in Company HTT's processes and procedures has always been hotly contested and contended against by the union and the employees. What can ameliorate this?
   a. Management ceasing from deriding the union.
   b. Consistent and solicitous communication.
   c. Management preparation for contention and resignations.
   d. Taking steps to remove the union and its representatives.

413. The creation, retention and distribution of organisational knowledge is termed as;
   a. Knowledge retention.
   b. Knowledge technology
   c. Knowledge management.
   d. Knowledge development.

414. Which of these knowledge management methods is recommended for an informal and spontaneous organisation?
   a. Best-practice standards.
   b. Technology solutions.
   c. Expert Registers.
   d. Communities of practice.

415. An expert register can be defined as;
   a. A register that lists the corporate experts for recognition purposes.
   b. A directory of the names and areas of expertise of employees that is updated and utilized by management.
   c. A register of expert employees for outsourcing and income generation
   d. A register of the names and areas of expertise of employees who can be contacted to help provide solutions.

416. All these are true about After-action evaluations except;

a. It is a post-mortem review.
b. It helps determine what knowledge can be retained.
c. <u>It is self-organized and spontaneous.</u>
d. It is conducted to determine what worked and what didn't work.

417. The goal of a Knowledge Management System (KMS) is all these except;
   a. Easy access to information.
   b. Accuracy and verification of information.
   c. <u>A robust customer database.</u>
   d. Capture and storage of organizational knowledge.

418. Peter Senge identified 5 disciplines of a learning organization, which of the following is not one of the disciplines;
   a. Personal Mastery.
   b. System Thinking.
   c. <u>Six Sigma.</u>
   d. Mental Models.

419. OD techno-structural interventions include all these except;
   a. <u>Team Learning</u>.
   b. Total Quality Management.
   c. Six Sigma.
   d. High Involvement Organizations.

420. DMAIC refers to the following except;
   a. DMAIC means Define, Measure, Analyze, Improve and Control.
   b. It is the Six Sigma methodology.
   c. <u>It was developed by the HR department of Apple in the 1980s.</u>
   d. It helps to find more precise way to increase quality standards.

421. Process owner is a structure level in;
   a. Process control chart.
   b. <u>Six Sigma.</u>
   c. Total Quality Management.
   d. Communities of Practice.

422. The RET organization encourages employees to design their work processes and empowers them to take actions to complete their work, it also holds them accountable for their results. The CEO, D. Douglas says the company has a flat hierarchy and self-directed work teams. The RET organization is a;
   a. Knowledge management organization.
   b. <u>High-Involvement Organization.</u>
   c. Human Process organization.

d. Spontaneous organization.

423. The 80/20 rule that helps to point out the areas of concern that will provide the greatest return when corrected is;
   a. Histogram
   b. Pareto chart.
   c. Stratification.
   d. Cause and effect diagram.

424. Edward Lawler identified four elements needed to create an High Involvement Organisation, which of these elements is not one of Lawler's elements?
   a. Information.
   b. Knowledge.
   c. Power.
   d. Development.

425. OD interventions directed at developing competencies at the individual level are called;
   a. Human Process Interventions.
   b. Strategic Interventions.
   c. Human Resource Interventions.
   d. Human Change Interventions.

426. Team building, Conflict resolution, Supervisory training and Emotional intelligence are examples of;
   a. Human Resource Development.
   b. Organization Development.
   c. Human Process Interventions.
   d. Human strategic interventions.

427. The HR Manager of GRT company has established that the 2016 goal of the HR team is to align employees more closely with organizational goals, focus on the attainment of objectives and raise the bar on quality of performance. The HR Manager intends to practice which of the following?
   a. Management by Performance
   b. Management by Objective.
   c. Management Interventions.
   d. Human Resource Management

428. Developing diversity programs, reward systems and hiring procedures that attract people with the required KSAs are examples of;
   a. Human Process Interventions.
   b. Human Resource Management Interventions.
   c. Human Resource Development.

d. Human Resource Performance.

429. ADDIE stands for;
   a. <u>Analysis, Design, Development, Implementation and Evaluation.</u>
   b. Analysis, Decide, Develop, Implement, Evaluate.
   c. Assessment, Design, Development, Implementation and Evaluation.
   d. Assessment, Develop, Disseminate, Implement and Evaluation.

430. A budget approach that requires that every expense be justified is called?
   a. Bottom-up budgeting
   b. <u>Zero-based budgeting</u>
   c. Historical budgeting.
   d. Parallel budgeting.

431. Which of the following accounting terms is defined inaccurately?
   a. <u>Budget - Liabilities plus Equity.</u>
   b. Equity - value of business to owners after all liabilities have been paid.
   c. Assets - Tangible or intangible items of value owned by the business.
   d. Accrued expense - Expenses that have been incurred but not yet paid.

432. Which of the following is not defined as a major life activity by the ADA?
   a. Driving.
   b. <u>Participating.</u>
   c. Personal hygiene.
   d. Speaking.

433. An affirmative action plan section that states the demographic information for the labor market related to a protected group is under what component?
   a. <u>Comparison of incumbency to availability.</u>
   b. Action-oriented programs.
   c. Periodic internal audits.
   d. Placement goals.

434. "Back pay awards cannot be a part of compensatory damages". Which legislation determined this?
   a. <u>Civil Rights Act of 1991.</u>
   b. Equal Employment Opportunity Act of 1972.
   c. Rehabilitation Act of 1973.
   d. Title VII of 1964.

435. A business structure where partners only invest but do not participate in daily operations is called?
   a. General partnership.

b. Joint venture.
   c. <u>Limited partnership.</u>
   d. Limited liability partnership.

436. Which of the following is true about job enrichment;
   a. It is a job design method.
   b. It involves assigning new responsibilities and developing new skills and abilities.
   c. It includes job factors such as autonomy and feedback.
   d. **<u>All of the above.</u>**

437. Skill variety, task identity, task significance are all factors of;
   a. Job enlargement.
   b. **<u>Job enrichment.</u>**
   c. Job productivity.
   d. Job evaluation.

438. Sue handles the bookkeeping of her organisation. Recently, additional tasks have been added to her role as the bookkeeper. Sue is not particularly pleased as the additional tasks do not result in a corresponding increase in pay. Sue's role has undergone;
   a. Skill variety
   b. Task variety.
   c. <u>Job enlargement.</u>
   d. Job enhancement.

439. Jane has over 10 years experience in HR. Upon Allen's request, Jane teaches and guides Allen who is a HR management trainee. She has helped Allen as a counselor on the workplace and gives valuable career advice. Allen can refer to Jane as his?
   a. Coach.
   b. **<u>Mentor.</u>**
   c. Facilitator.
   d. Guide.

440. The Temple Inc.has undergone significant changes due to the rapid rate of technological development in its industry. The CEO has requested that a set of young, tech-savvy talent be employed to help the older co-workers understand and adapt to the technological changes. The young talent will serve as;
   a. Mentors.
   b. Coaches.
   c. <u>Reverse mentors.</u>
   d. Tech facilitators.

441. A monetary sum paid to Jim, an employee at an IT company based upon a management judgement made at the end of the year is called …… pay?

a. Formula-based.
b. Pity-based.
c. Service-based.
d. Discretionary.

442. Ann needs to represent the percentage of turnover for the last ten years. What tool will be most relevant for this?
a. Control chart.
b. Histogram.
c. Pareto chart.
d. Check sheet.

443. The most relevant aspect of creating a strong safety culture is?
a. Allowing and acting on OSHA safety complaints.
b. Involving staff and top management in the creation of safety policies.
c. Providing employee incentives for meeting safety goals.
d. Ensure employee opinions are not disseminated.

444. Which of this is true about the OSHA's General policy?
a. Employers provide hazard-free environments.
b. Employees report unsafe working conditions to OSHA.
c. Employees need not come to a workplace that is unsafe.
d. Employers file annual reports of safety issues with the EEOC.

445. The main reason employees join unions is;
a. Have a sense of belonging.
b. Stand up to the excesses of management.
c. Activate their leadership skills.
d. Guarantee a safe and secure work environment.

446. What is the weighted average of $2,000 (2 incumbents), $3,000 (1 incumbent), $3,500 (2 incumbents) and $4,000 (1 incumbent).
a. 2,500.
b. 3,000
c. 3,125.
d. 3,500.

447. Union recognition is usually as a result of:
a. Voluntary recognition by employer.
b. 80% recognition by employees.
c. An NLRB-ordered election.
d. When an employer commits a maximum of 3 ULPs.

448. Which of the following is not an intervention strategy of B.F. Skinner's Operant Conditioning?
   a. Positive reinforcement.
   b. Binding reinforcement.
   c. Negative reinforcement.
   d. Extinction.

449. A benchmark job can be defined as;
   a. A job used in the external labour market for setting wages.
   b. A job used as the mode of job evaluation.
   c. A job in the middle of the pay structure for its class.
   d. A job in the entry-level job in its class.

450. In what circumstance must an organization set a placement goal?
   a. Inability to determine the ethnicity of its applicants.
   b. Where an adverse impact in hiring practices is re-discovered.
   c. Employs less women or minorities than is available in the labour market.
   d. Only an organisation in the OFCCP's red list is required to have a placement goal.

451. Ann has indicated that she is interested in an announced opening in her organisation. The announced opening is best described as;
   a. Job bidding.
   b. Job posting.
   c. Skill training.
   d. Career planning.

452. Which of the following is against the regulations of the NLRA?
   a. Salting.
   b. Arbitrary expositions.
   c. Employer domination of unions.
   d. Associative bargaining.

453. The Vroom expectancy theory (1964) stipulates that;
   a. Employees work better in a team than under coercion.
   b. Employee's effort is related to the likelihood of perceived success.
   c. Experiences acquired through life motivate people.
   d. Operant conditioning is more effective with negative reinforcement.

454. Which of these is the most effective for union organizing and campaign?
   a. Salting.
   b. Leafleting.
   c. Inside organizing.
   d. Picketing.

455. Gregg, an employee at PTT Inc. has a son who is no longer eligible for coverage under the company's health scheme plan. The COBRA regulation states that the Gregg's son is eligible for how many months of insurance continuation?
   a. <u>36.</u>
   b. 18.
   c. 24.
   d. 40.

456. When a group of employees patrol the entrance of an organisation in order to get the employer to recognize the union as the employee's representative for collective bargaining purposes, this is known as:
   a. Picketing.
   b. Organizational picketing.
   c. <u>Recognitional picketing.</u>
   d. Publicity picketing.

457. According to the FLSA, exempt status would include a manager who;
   a. Receives overtime pay only once a year despite busy periods.
   b. Makes less than $455 per week.
   c. <u>Directs 6 people and has hiring and firing responsibility.</u>
   d. Is docked for less than 2 full days away from the job.

458. A union intends to picket an organization to attract employees to authorize the union to represent them with the employer. However, a representation petition has not been filed within 30 days of the picketing start date? Is this picketing legal?
   a. Yes, the union has a legal right to picket.
   b. <u>No, a representation petition has to be filed within 30 days of the start of the picketing.</u>
   c. All picketing are illegal without the NLRB's permission.
   d. All picketings are legal by the LMRA.

459. HR's strategic role in the organization is best described as;
   a. <u>Influence and affect management's view on organizational change.</u>
   b. Institute interpersonal relations such as mentors and coaches.
   c. Ensure compliance with management's dictates and keep the union on a leash.
   d. Quel resistance to organizational change.

460. A pre-election hearing has been constituted to resolve issues between an employer and the union before an election to determine union representation takes place. This election is called;
   a. Consent election.
   b. Hearing election.
   c. <u>Directed election.</u>

d. Adjudicated election.

461. During an election campaign, both parties are allowed to do which of the following;
   a. Campaign in the polling booths outside election hours.
   b. Distribute fliers in the polling booths outside election hours.
   c. Solicit individuals' votes outside the polling area outside election hours.
   d. Solicit individuals' votes outside the polling area while voting occurs.

462. An employer is required to provide an Excelsior list within 7 days of an union election, what is an Excelsior list?
   a. A list of management personnel.
   b. A list containing the names and addresses of all employees in the bargaining unit.
   c. A list containing the names of all employees interested in union representation.
   d. A list of names and addresses of all employees.

463. When a qualified white candidate is denied an employment opportunity due to preference given to a member of a protected group, this is known as;
   a. Undue hardship.
   b. Reasonable accommodation.
   c. Affirmative Action.
   d. Reverse discrimination.

464. Employees want to know what makes them eligible to vote in a union election. Which of the following is not correct;
   a. Employees must have worked during the pay period preceding the election.
   b. Employees must not have engaged in company picketing.
   c. Employees must be employed by the business on the day of the election.
   d. Employees must not be in management

465. Which of the following gave union members the right to secret ballot elections for union officers and the right to sue the union?
   a. Labour-management relation act.
   b. Railway labour act.
   c. National labour relation act.
   d. Labour-management reporting & disclosure act (LMRDA).

466. Which of these is a prerequisite to developing a recruitment strategy for an organisation's operations?
   a. Environmental scanning.
   b. Turnover analysis.
   c. Equity technique.
   d. Benchmarking.

467. How many votes must the union receive to certify it as the bargaining representative for employees in the unit;
   a. 50%
   b. 60% plus one vote.
   c. <u>50% plus one vote.</u>
   d. 51%.

468. Which of the following action is taken in the strategic formulation phase?
   a. Creating a company culture.
   b. <u>Deciding the organization's mission.</u>
   c. Creating a zero-based budget.
   d. Conducting communication focus group.

469. Which of these explanations of union election bars is inaccurate?
   a. Blocking-charge Bar - An election petition is barred when there is a pending ULP charge.
   b. Voluntary-Recognition Bar - An election is barred because the employer has voluntarily recognized the union.
   c. <u>Contract Bar - An election is barred because the employment contract indicates so.</u>
   d. Statutory Bar - An election is barred because a valid election took place in the preceding 12-month period.

470. How will HR evaluate the effectiveness of its programs vs. their financial result?
   a. Delphi technique.
   b. <u>Cost-benefit analysis</u>
   c. Constructive correlation.
   d. Average analysis.

471. When employees decide to remove a union security clause and 30% or more petition the NLRB for approval of the removal, this is known as;
   a. Decertification.
   b. De-representation.
   c. <u>Deauthorization.</u>
   d. Bargaining.

472. The most critical stage in outsourcing to a contractor is;
   a. Establishing deadlines.
   b. <u>Analyzing needs.</u>
   c. Implementing the outsourced proposal.
   d. Determine the compensable factors.

473. Competitive bargaining that emphasises on "winner takes all' is known as;
   a. <u>Positional bargaining.</u>
   b. Principles bargaining.

c. Collective bargaining.
d. Finite bargaining.

474. The following questions are relevant to strategic planning except?
   a. How will the organisation get there?
   b. Where does the organisation want to go?
   c. Where is the organisation now?
   d. Who should lead the strategic process?

475. Which of the following best explains Interest-based bargaining?
   a. Both parties are antagonistic to each other's position.
   b. Both parties have harmonious interests.
   c. Both parties are involved in hard bargaining.
   d. Both parties have parallel interests.

476. A motivation concept which states that experiences acquired throughout people's lives motivates them in Achievement, Affiliation or Power is called;
   a. Acquired Needs Theory - 1961.
   b. Hierarchy of Needs - 1954.
   c. ERG Theory - 1969.
   d. Expectancy Theory - 1964.

477. A test can be regarded as valid for an clerical applicant if it;
   a. Measures managerial ability.
   b. Measures for a receptive and pleasant character.
   c. Measures typing accuracy and speed.
   d. Measures strategic thinking and application.

478. Bargaining which involves several unions representing several bargaining units in a company is called;
   a. Multi-unit bargaining.
   b. Principled bargaining.
   c. Multi union bargaining.
   d. None of the above.

479. The Path-Goal Theory of 1971 is based on the following leadership styles except?
   a. Directive - specifies what is to be done.
   b. Maturity - leader achieves the goals himself.
   c. Supportive - provides encouragement.
   d. Participative - involves the group in the decision-making process.

480. The RED company has a single union which bargains with only one employer, this is known as;

a. Direct bargaining.
   b. <u>Single-unit bargaining.</u>
   c. Indirect bargaining.
   d. Parallel bargaining.

481. When a union negotiates with one employer at a time in order to use the gains made from the previous negotiations as a base for the next employer, this is known as;
   a. Zero-sum game bargaining.
   b. Adversarial bargaining.
   c. <u>Parallel bargaining.</u>
   d. Gain-based bargaining.

482. Which of these project life-cycle phases involves the establishing of a project timeline?
   a. Closing.
   b. <u>Planning.</u>
   c. Initiation.
   d. Executing.

483. The reserved right doctrine means;
   a. <u>Rights not covered in agreements are the sole responsibility of management.</u>
   b. Rights covered in agreements are the sole responsibility of the union.
   c. Rights not covered in agreements are the sole responsibility of the union.
   d. All rights are the sole responsibility of the NLRB.

484. A leadership style that provides no direction or guidance to group members is called?
   a. Coaching.
   b. Democratic.
   c. <u>Laissez-faire.</u>
   d. Transformational.

485. The GET company has identified topics for negotiation with the union. Which of the following topics are illegal for discussion?
   a. Wages and hours.
   b. <u>Hot-cargo clauses.</u>
   c. Terms of employment.
   d. Negotiation of agreements.

486. Employees seeking whistleblower protection must provide *prima facie* evidence of violation. What are the elements of a *prima facie* violation?
   a. The employee was engaged in a protected activity.
   b. The employee suffered an unfavorable employment action.
   c. Sufficient evidence exists to show that a contributing factor to the unfavorable action was the employee's participation in the protected activity.

d. All of the above.

488. The following are advantages of a diverse workforce except?
   a. They are more conflict-prone.
   b. It increases the candidate pool.
   c. Creativity.
   d. Customer attraction.

489. Learning Management Systems (LMS) streamlines the administration of employee trainings. Which of the following is not one of the uses of the LMS?
   a. Provide self-service functions.
   b. Identify skill-development needs.
   c. Enroll employees in required courses.
   d. Maintain discrimination investigation information.

490. A quantitative analysis tool which measures the relationship between one variable against another variable for prediction purposes is called?
   a. Trend analysis.
   b. Simple linear regression.
   c. Weighted Average.
   d. Central Tendency.

491. Business Impact measures show how an HR activity adds value to the bottom line. Which of these is an example of a business impact measurement?
   a. Return on Investment.
   b. Cost/Benefit Analysis.
   c. Judgemental forecast.
   d. A and B.

492. Tactical Accountability Measures provide information for evaluating the effectiveness of HR programs. Which of the following is NOT a tactical accountability measure?
   a. Training cost per employee.
   b. OSH Act Review.
   c. Cost per hire.
   d. Absenteeism and sick leave frequency.

493. The following are steps to the scientific method of primary research except?
   a. Identify a problem.
   b. Create a team from the collective bargaining department.
   c. Test the hypothesis.
   d. Draw conclusions on verified data.

494. A situational theory of leadership which considers two aspects of leadership; concern for people and concern for production is called;
   a. Hersey-Blanchard theory.
   b. Contingency theory.
   c. Blake-Mouton Managerial Grid.
   d. J.Stacey theory.

495. A manager who views employees as lazy and in need of constant direction to complete assignments is best described as a;
   a. Theory W manager.
   b. Theory X manager.
   c. Theory Y manager.
   d. Slave-master.

496. Which of the following are included in a Request For Proposal?
   a. Brief description of organization.
   b. Overview of project and summary of needs.
   c. Detailed project description.
   d. All of the above.

497. Which of the following communication methods is bottom-up?
   a. Newsletters.
   b. Intranet.
   c. Union meetings.
   d. Posters.

498. Malcolm Knowles described five characteristics of andragogy. What is andragogy?
   a. Study of how adults learn.
   b. Study of how HR influences employee decisions.
   c. Study of HR Return on Investment.
   d. Study of Safety in the workplace.

499. Which of the following characteristics of andragogy by Malcolm Knowles is incorrectly described?
   a. Self-concept - Move from dependency to self-direction.
   b. Experience - Wealth of knowledge built from classroom learning only.
   c. Readiness to learn - Interest in relevance of information.
   d. Motivation to learn - learning is based on personal needs rather than expectations of others.

500. The following are motivation theories except?
   a. Maslow Hierarchy of Needs -1954.
   b. Clayton Alderfer's ERG Theory - 1969.

c. Victor Vroom's Expectancy Theory - 1964.
d. <u>Hersey-Blanchard Theory - 1977</u>.

Made in the USA
San Bernardino, CA
05 November 2016